Money or Santa Claus: Which is Real?

A Special Theory of Economic Relativity

WILLIAM BERNSTEIN

ISBN: 9781092642910
Library of Congress Control Number: 2017946991
LCCN Imprint Name: **Charlotte, NC**

For Kim and Kam

PART I

What is Money?

"Make as much as you can. For as long as you can. Whoever has the most when he dies, WINS."

Other People's Money
-- play by Jerry Sterner
film adaptation by Alvin Sargent

1

What is money?

Although "What is money?" might seem like a fairly obvious question, it's actually extremely difficult to answer. Money is one of the most abstract concepts we humans use. Sure, we believe money is quite concrete; after all, I use money to pay for anything I need (and very often for what I just want).

But think about it. What a strange concept that is: "I can buy a certain dinner with a certain amount of money."

Nor is it that simple. I can buy a certain dinner, only because some value is given to the dinner. If we start talking about a bottle of wine, that value becomes more obviously subjective and variable. And the "value" given to the dinner or the wine is in terms of how much I—and all the other few billion people on earth— want the dinner.

So, does money represent a certain number of dinners? Or a certain type of dinner? Which holds the value —the money, or the dinner? Here we are saying that money is worth a certain number of dinners (or maybe a certain percent of one dinner.).

We can't carry dinners with us, so we carry money. Or at least we used to carry money — or what used to be money, when humans first invented this concept. We've refined the concept so that today, we often don't bother to carry

3

money. We have credit cards. Sometimes we don't even need the cards, as long as we know the number of the card.

This is getting complicated. We have a number, which represents an "account." But what is that? Even the account is just a concept, some ethereal "data," stored on a computer somewhere. So, I don't have any actual money, or dinners, or anything, in the bank. The bank has my account number, which represents – What?

My employer tells the bank that I earned a certain amount of money, which the employer is transferring from their account to my account. Nobody took any dinners, or gold (which, after all, is just a different substance – just like the food of which the dinner is made) and put them in my account.

Somebody just transferred some numbers from one computer to another.

This is a modern example of a transaction that has been taking place since people recognized that some goods were worth more than others, and found a way to represent that value. This was necessary as we began to develop from hunter-gatherer groups toagriculturally based civilizations. But in this modern example, we are able to perceive more easily just how abstract our concept of money is.

Once we step outside the paradigm that we carry with us from those days when humans first started assigning a value on things; when we stop and look at the whole arena of transactions in which we all engage; and if we begin to ask fundamental questions… then the whole mess doesn't make an awful lot of sense.

You might be thinking, "Money has worked great for us for thousands of years." But is that true?

If we are honest, we must admit there have been problems. As you read this treatise, you'll be reminded of vast numbers of problems that we've encountered and are continuing to encounter.

Maybe we should get back to the more relevant question; one that our species has asked since we've existed as *homo sapiens,* whether we are defining methods of physical labor, shelter, or survival.

All our innovations flow from this question:

Is this the best we can do?

A fundamental element helping form the basis of how we view the world and our life in the world is that we think of money as something we can exchange for things we need, things we want—material objects as well as services: Food, shelter, clothing, health, transportation, entertainment, and so on. Money is nothing on its own, but it circulates from one person in exchange for his or her goods (the produce the person buy in a market) to the next person for a service (carry my produce on your mule) to the next person (a miller who sells flour to the mule owner), and so on. In modern examples, we order a book online; and pay Amazon to send a courier to deliver it to our door; and the courier transfers that deposit to the bank so she or he can buy groceries at the supermarket with his or her credit/debit card.

Why is money needed for those things? Because the people who work to provide those goods and services also need money to buy the goods and services they need.

This seems like a logical, self-perpetuating system. Money (which we're still trying to understand) is itself represented by a number, which goes into a person's account, so the person can then use that number to get what they need or want.

In this way the money, or at least the numbers that represent the money that represents something else, moves from one computer to another, circling around.

In recent decades, as it circles through its course, more of it seems to end up in fewer people's accounts.

My mother used to use the expression, "Do we eat to live, or do we live to eat?" We're asking another, broader version of the question here: Should we work for money, or should money work for us?

2

It's Not Real

At one time General Motors was the largest company in the United States.In 2008, it was failing. The discussion in financial markets became an analysis of how the finances of the company should have been managed differently, and how the contracts with the employees' unions affected finances, and so on.

Only the people who bought cars seemed to feel that the problem began as more than how the finances of the company were managed, but rather that the quality of the cars might have lessened. Some felt that other cars handled better, looked better, were more comfortable, got better mileage, and had more innovative accessories. Ford became aware of similar problems and started making better cars; so Ford saved itself by the oldest principle in capitalism: improve the product, sell a better product.

This fundamental principle is often forgotten by those whose only goal is to move money.

Our current system has become so perverted that people tasked with moving money—with investing in others' projects— have come to believe that money is the only object. No one remembers that money represents something else, that it has no value independent of other things.

Throughout history, most people believed that the reason for making money was to be able to live in a reasonable manner. There were always people, a tiny number of people, who were able to use the income generated through others' work, or even from others' money, to create a much richer lifestyle for themselves than the lifestyle which most people experienced, but in today's world a new paradigm has emerged.

This new paradigm is best described as a view of the world, of our lives, as taking place for the main purpose of making more and more money, acquiring more and more things. This has mistakenly come to be viewed as the basic foundation of the financial system known as capitalism. This is, however, a perversion of that system that is blindly accepted as somehow necessary for democracy, a building block of freedom. More money, more possessions, is viewed as a birthright; synonymous with the pursuit of happiness.

The ultimate dishonesty in this perception is the assumption that this "common birthright" is most deserved by those who attain it (whether through actual endeavor or inheritance or other means), rather than by the great majority of people. That is, if you don't have a tremendous amount of money, it is because you don't deserve it. You are thus not entitled to it.

This philosophy—sometimes termed "Economic Darwinism"—entitles those who achieve wealth to justify to themselves the abuse of the system that has continually increased the percentage of wealth under their control.

Perhaps we should wonder about economic evolution: the survival of the fittest. If I can defeat you financially, I deserve more money. I won; survival of the fittest.

Is Capitalism really financial Darwinism? Is it correct to assume that those who make the most must *deserve* to make the most?

Let's examine the economy of the United States. Our economy has at various times been in great debt, and at times had a surplus.

What does this mean? Whose money is it that is borrowed? Where is it? What does it *represent?* That last word is always the magic word: *represent.* Remember—money has no basic value except as it represents something else, something of value. A bit later we will take a brief look at an example of this issue in its extremity, the "debt crisis" that was purported to exist in the United States in mid 2011 and the clear-cut example of the relativity and absurdity of our modern perspective on national and international economic structures that were shown by that "crisis."

First, let's scale back to a single dollar. What is the "something of value" that a dollar bill represents? The U.S. used to link its currency to gold. All dollars in circulation were supported by an equal amount of gold, held at Fort Knox. That's not the case anymore, but even when it was the case, what did the gold *represent?* The value of gold, like anything else, is only in relation to what it can buy.

Everything is related to something else. We humans assign value.

So, the nation's wealth – that is, the wealth handled by the government of the nation – is determined by figures on a piece of paper, or in a computer. At times the country spends more than it receives through taxes and other means. We all believe that we shouldn't do that, although individuals and families borrow money, too. We buy houses using a mortgage, we charge things we buy on credit, etc. Even if we pay off the credit card each month, and pay no interest, we're still borrowing the money from the credit card company until we pay it back.

But in the case of the government, the sources from which they borrow money are a complicated assortment of entities, many of them part of the government itself. And a part of it is from the people that loan the government money by purchasing bonds. It comes from somewhere and goes somewhere, but whose money is it? Who actually *owns* the money?

Ownership becomes a complicated concept, because the government represents the people of the nation, and the money is often coming from abstract entities that are functioning within the framework of the assemblage of people who make up the country.

So the government spends more than it takes in, and tells us it is in debt. What would happen if the government said that money was only a concept? What if the governments of the world adopted a different construct in order to function?

This may seem like a leap, but a prime example of the unreality of money—the fact that it is hardly more real than vapor or ether—is the concept of government bonds. This is an illustration of the interdependence of money, of the circularity of what we view as an economic structure, of the fact that money depends on itself in a very strange way.

People often feel that the safest investment they can make is in government savings bonds. People "buy" governments bonds in return for the interest on those bonds and the fact that their money is being "held" by the government. The government, on the other hand, views this as a "loan" from the people who invest in the bonds. So the government has borrowed money from people, guaranteeing to repay that money at some point, and to pay interest in return for having their money for a certain period of time.

What is the source of the money which people "lend" to the government in the form of bonds that are purchased; where does it come from? Who guarantees what that money represents—what it is worth—in the first place? The government does, of course. So, the government of a country—in the shape of the institution represented by the treasury of that country—is issuing money, guaranteeing that the money is worth a certain amount. The people to whom that money goes then, in turn, purchase bonds from that treasury (that government) with the guarantee that the government will repay that money. Meanwhile, the government spends the money. If the government itself borrows too much money, then perhaps it can't pay back the money.

Whose money is it in the first place? Who guarantees what that dollar is worth? Is it not the government that guarantees it? Why does the government then need to "borrow" it back in the first place?

The government issued the money and proclaimed, "Here is something that I say is 'worth' X amount. Here is money." Where did the money come from? What is the bedrock, the foundation, of the value of the money? It is, of course, the government, which issues (creates) the money, and then asks people *to loan it back*.

Imagine that there's lots of snow on the ground. I make some snowballs, and roll them into many different size snowballs; one of them into a giant snowball big enough to start making a snowman. I have distributed these snowballs into the community, and when you work, you are paid in snowballs, which I have said are worth something. Anything you want to buy can be bought using snowballs, because they have a certain "value". You've accumulated quite a few snowballs, which you've rolled into one big one. You loan me that one, in return for my giving you some small ones each year, and my promising that in a certain number of years I'll return your big snow ball to you.

But the big snowball, the medium snowballs, and the small snowballs, are worth something only because I support them and everyone trusts what I say is their value. If we have no independent foundation, if each snowball depends only on another snowball with no guarantee that the temperature will remain cold enough, then then global climate change is not going to bode well for us or for those snowballs.

To use another analogy, if we are like the two people jumping out of the plane depending on each other for support with no parachute, things are not going to end well.

We depend on the government to support the value of the money, just as you depended on me to maintain the giant refrigerator that supported the value of the snowballs. As soon as I start saying that the value of the snowballs is not determined by something independent of the snowballs, we could both be in trouble. In the case of the snowballs, of course, we are both dependent on the giant refrigerator that is the weather.

But in the case of the financial system of a government, or of the world, as soon as we say that those systems are dependent on entities outside of government —government which represents, after all, human beings—that exist only with the abstract, ethereal purpose of producing something as truly meaningless as money, then the government has abrogated its responsibility and jumped from the plane holding onto its people, even as the people are holding onto the government, without a parachute.

Two things that depend on each other, that don't have a third, objective "something" on which they can depend for their support, are like those two people jumping out of an airplane holding on to each other for support, without a parachute. None of us wants to be those people. We have depended upon this artificial structure to function; but many of us are starting to realize the insubstantiality of this. The emperor has no clothes.

We must find a better way.

3

Was money ever real?

Until 1971 the value of currency in the United States was based on gold, or what was referred to as the "gold standard." Gold was assumed to have a certain intrinsic value, whereas paper bills or coins could only be valued in terms of the value of that gold. In today's world there remains a set of people who still believe that economic structure was healthier, and that the U.S. should return to the gold standard.

Unlike paper, gold is not something that is produced by human beings (side note: Sir Isaac Newton studied and believed in alchemy, and he tried to create gold). That makes the value of gold a bit less mutable; but what actually determines its value? Human beings determine that value, and that value is measured in terms of what humans use as "money", whether that is dollars, yen, francs, or any other term. Just like money, gold can buy a certain amount of that which is necessary and/or useful for life. Because there is a limited supply of gold, people have the impression that an objective value can be placed on it. But that value is entirely subjective, and is determined by a quantity, by a number, by a significance that we set.

The idea of assigning an arbitrary value to anything versus its relativity to gold helped to bring humans to a point in our evolution that enabled us to form societies.

15

Hard Cash

Fast forward to the 21st century. In 2011, the United States one cent coin, the penny, worth one cent, actually cost two-and-a-half (2.5) cents to make. The five-cent coin, the nickel, worth five cents, cost ten (10) cents to make. Think about that for a minute: if you consider money to have real value, if you want to make a penny, you can do that—by investing two-and-a-half pennies. If you want a nickel, it will cost you a dime to make. But it will cost you two nickels to get a dime.

In recent decades, these coins have cost more than their value. Think about what that means. What does a penny or nickel represent? They *represent* one cent or five cents, right? Where does the money come from to make a penny or a nickel? If you have to use two nickels to make a nickel, how can anyone say that what a nickel is worth? What does it even mean to say that it costs two-and-a-half cents to make something that represents one cent? Once the process becomes that abstract, we must realize that we can do better.

To bring this picture into clearer focus, let's talk about cash, and what it represents. Some corporations have "cash reserves" of millions—or even billions—of dollars. What would happen if the financial officer of one of those corporations walked into their bank and asked to withdraw a billion dollars? Not in the form of a check representing some number—but in the form of a billion dollars in cash.

The very concept is so absurd that it is beyond our comprehension. Yet, that billion dollars in cash is what is represented by the numbers in the bank account of some corporations. Where is that "cash"—the money? What are we actually talking about? Whatever anyone may tell you, the fact is that no one knows.

Inflation happens

Inflation shows how relative the value of money is. If money had intrinsic value, how could that value change? But one dollar bought a certain amount of bread in 1900, less in 1970, less in 1990, less in 2010. Is the bread worth more, or is the money worth less? Does it seem to you that the "value" of basic products seems to remain a constant even as the value of money fluctuates?

To answer this question, let's talk about economic relativity.

For a few hundred years scientists operated with an understanding of the universe based largely on the theories of Isaac Newton, a truly brilliant man. From the Newtonian perspective, the motions of bodies in the universe, the flow of time, the structure of space, were all fixed from an objective perspective.

Albert Einstein gave us a more accurate understanding of the basic foundations of the universe through his Special and General Theories of Relativity. Time and space exist relative to each other. Energy is relative to mass and motion. Then gravity was also shown to be relative, rather than an independently fixed entity. These concepts became extremely confusing to most of us, but nonetheless have been objectively proven to be more accurate; more based in reality.

Since the human race began using money, whichever economic system an individual nation used—capitalist, socialist, communist, or other—we have operated under the economic equivalent of a Newtonian model. Even as we learned about the universe, advanced in our understanding of human cultures, and made great leaps in medical technology, we have remained mired in this erroneously based assumption: That money has some independent, fixed, objectively verifiable value, just as Newtonian physics assumed an independent status of the objects in the universe.

4

What is the Capital in "Capitalism"?

Much of the basis for the financial system that the economy of the United States operates in has its roots in the economic philosophy of Adam Smith, who in 1776 published *The Wealth of Nations*, an important book that helped establish, in the eyes of many, capitalism as the foundation of our economic system. According to The Adam Smith Institute (www.adamsmith.org):

"Building up capital is an essential condition for economic progress. By saving some of what we produce instead of immediately consuming it, we can invest in new, dedicated, labour-saving equipment. The more we invest, the more efficient our production becomes. It is a virtuous circle. Thanks to this growth of capital, prosperity becomes an expanding pie: everyone becomes richer."

What we call "capitalism" today is, however, very much at odds with what Adam Smith would have called capitalism.

The entity whose only goal is to enable a few people to accumulate more "bullion" (bullion was Smith's word for money; referring to gold, of course) is anathema to the very concept of capitalism. Yet, that word—capitalism—is constantly used in almost a spiritual manner as the basis for a system that focuses on the accumulation of bullion and material wealth.

In his book, Smith berated those to whom the possession of bullion was the determination of their wealth. To Smith, wealth—or capital—represented the creation of products by a labor force who in turn consumed the products. To put it very simply: people make things, and people buy things. According to Smith, this circulation represents the wealth of a nation; the wealth of a nation—let's remember that the title, the foundation of his book, was "The Wealth of Nations"—was not the amount of money (or bullion) that a nation has.

Is Wealth Measured in Possessions?

Smith spoke about "mercantilists," to whom *production* was the most important thing. Sound familiar? When you follow economic reports on TV or the Web or the radio, productivity is one of the key factors in determining the value of a company and, ultimately, the direction of the economy in general. Yet Smith argued against such a concept, maintaining that consumption, not production, is the goal of an economy. We talk about both today, and the financial reports also focus on consumption, but without realizing how we subvert one with the other.

Possessions did not define wealth, according to Smith. This would come as a shock to most of us who grew up in the 20th/21st century U.S.A. Smith, whose model is valued by us in our perception of the economic system of capitalism, would be horrified if he could see what is happening today in many nations that believe they are "capitalist."

Smith's definition of the function of a capitalist economic system says this: What is produced by laborers—the products or commodities—are for the purpose of consumption.

A sale is a mutually beneficial transaction.

It is the link between production and consumption that defines wealth.

"No society can surely be flourishing and happy of which by far the greater part of the numbers are poor and miserable." *The Wealth of Nations,* Adam Smith.

Almost a century after Smith's Wealth of Nations, Karl Marx argued that, although Smith described what was originally the way economic systems functioned, in such an economic system the principle goal of a person (or let us say, a corporation) becomes increased profit. Rather than production for the sake of consumption, the aim of production is for profit alone. According to this concept, this goal naturally leads to exploitation.

The treatise you are reading now makes the point that what Marx describes as "capitalism" is actually not what Smith talked about as capitalism; that thinkers such as Adam Smith, who defined the economic systems under which much of the world operates today, clearly believed that accumulation of wealth for its own sake was not a healthy function of an economy.

Yet, that appears to be the main function of that increasingly small number of people who today control an increasingly large percentage of the money in America. Let us be careful with the words we use— I didn't say they control a greater percentage of the "wealth" in America, only a greater percentage of the "money," or what Adam Smith called "bullion."

The realities of each of the economies functioning in today's world have elements of both Smith's theories and Marx's theories. Smith discussed the value of the goods produced in any economic system. Marx said that when considering value, the value of the work of the laborers who produce those goods must be taken into consideration. In today's world, employees have negotiated with employers to determine their worth and thus, their salaries. The battle is always re-fought, of course, with employers trying to get more from employees while paying lower wages, and employees trying to get more, believing their labor is worth more.

In all economic theories, various concepts determine function. But let us make the great leap that we should now be able to make. Let us consider the most basic ideas.

What is necessary for a person to live the sort of life that this planet is capable of sustaining? Not at a minimalist level, but at a level of real comfort. What determines whether a person should or should not be able to live that life?

"A nation is not made welthy by the childish accumulation of shiny metals, but it enriched by the economic prosperity of its people." *The Wealth of Nations,* Adam Smith

"Capital is money, capital is commodities. By virtue of it being value, it has acquired the occult ability to add value to itself. It brings forth living offspring, or, at the least, lays golden eggs." *On the Progress of Wealth,* Karl Marx

Most of those who work in the financial sector are not concerned with the broader issue of economic theory, but rather with the tools to increase money. This is the mathematics of economics, which is so easily tied to the simple concepts of "what will make more money."

Adam Smith criticized those who join forces to try to influence the government to do what will benefit their concerns. Today we would call one group of people who do that work lobbyists. It should interest everyone to know that the founder of capitalism would have been extremely critical of those who today claim to be practicing capitalism, who claim to believe in the model for which the foundation was laid by Adam Smith.

In fact, the economies of almost all modern industrialized nations are built on a structure that is increasingly determined by major corporate interests, rather than human interests. Somewhere along the way we lost sight of the fundamental, obvious principle that governments should function as a cohesive entity serving the people of the country.

Let's look at the stock market as an example. Those who invest in the stock market are buying part of a company; not much of it, but a tiny "share." When the idea of a company (something that is, as of this writing, still run by people) selling its shares to others first came about, the principle was that the company could get money that it needed to further its operations—its functioning— by giving the investor a share in the company in return for that money.

It started on a small scale, of course, relative to the world in which we live now. Today it's usually a different animal. People invest—put their money in the stock of a company—with the goal of making more money. Many of us invest in mutual funds, themselves run by companies that diversify the investment so that we usually don't have a clue about what percentage of what companies we "own".

The main difference between the stock market and gambling in Las Vegas is that in the long run with the stock market we have pretty decent odds of making money rather than losing money. But it's still a gamble, and the "house" is still making a lot more than we are, because as time passes, they make use of our money. Only in this case the house isn't a casino, it's a corporation. They're still making money from our willingness to gamble on a return from them.

But this gambling is legal— unless (or until) someone running the corporation does something they're not supposed to do.

Your goal, as a shareholder, is to make more money. The goal of the corporation is—theoretically—to make more money by producing the product or service that they are in business to produce. But the executives at the top of the company may have a different goal. Their goal may simply be to make more money in the short term for the company, which could mean for themselves, whatever that requires. More investment in the corporation, which may mean more money for them, may be determined by various seemingly abstract decisions. And that works for you, up to a point. The point at which it stops working is when the executives see the company losing money and bail out with their own huge payout that is received in spite of whatever damage has been done to the company.

When a society's main motivation for any gratification or sense of achievement is money, then in order for the individual to achieve his/her goal of getting money, the issue of what the company does may not be the most important thing.

In that case, does owning stocks sound like a gamble?

But this gamble is not for an enjoyable weekend in Vegas, taking in some great shows and having some good meals while you win or lose a bit at the tables. This gamble is for your life. This gamble is to help you pay your rent, your mortgage, put food on your table, send your children to school, plan your retirement, get the medical care you need if you are ill; in short, to make it possible for you to live.

And what is it that determines whether you win or lose in this gamble? The major investment firms that put other people's money in stocks make decisions on many factors. In the paradigm that has taken shape in today's world, only one of these factors is the actual quality of the product or service produced by a company, or even the extent to which those products or services are used by others. Instead, issues such as the debt of other nations, inflation, stagflation, unemployment, gross domestic product, and balance of trade might cause the stock in a particular company to go up or down.

5

Animal Spirits

One small example of this can be seen from what happened a day after a hurricane went through the east coast of the United States. In 2011 Hurricane Irene did not do as much damage as anticipated. Because of this, on the first working day after the hurricane went through New York City, at the august New York stock exchange, the Dow Jones Industrial average gained in value. The short-term value of many corporations increased. This was not based on anything to do with real financial transactions or work in any of these corporations. It happened, essentially, because traders' emotions were affected in a positive way.

Since what often determines major market fluctuations in today's world is based on algorithms in the brains of large computers, of course, we can never be sure of what precipitates positive or negative market moves.

Sometimes economists recognize the effect of such events, however, calling this phenomenon "animal spirits."

Naturally, these spirits are equally vulnerable to bad moods.

Let's look at another example of the absurdity of the manner in which national economic systems operate. At times we may hear from news reports, quoting economists, that people are not spending enough, so that is a sign that the economy is not growing quickly enough, and thus the economy is in bad shape. At the same time another economic analysis might be remarking that the rate of saving is not sufficient because people are not saving enough. Either way, it's not good.

And that perspective, that things are "not good" economically, causes ripple effects throughout a nation, as members of the society seem to acquire a sort of economic malaise during which people take on a pessimistic outlook and tell others how bad things are.

To what extent, then, is the worth of a company measured in terms of the actual work it produces? And to what extent is it measured by world conditions over which the company has no influence, but which play a significant role in influencing the funds invested in that company?

This presents another contradiction, a true indication of how abstract the economic structure representing our own worth has become. If an individual tried to engage in schemes such as these to make money, that person would be arrested. In fact, many people have been arrested for investment schemes that are viewed as illegal if carried out by an individual. But such schemes carried out by a large enough organization only earn it more money.

I don't mean to criticize large business operations. They exist to do a certain work that is an integral part of society, as well as to make money for their investors.

It is the *structure of the system* that has allowed things to become so perverted.

With globalization, the structure has become even more abstract and unrelated to the corporations whose shares are traded around the world. Each market in each nation is dependent upon the markets in every other nation, which means that each individual company is dependent upon what happens to the value of the shares of other companies. If anything unpleasant—or anything perceived as detrimental to investment (not investment in a particular company, but investment in the "market" as a whole)— occurs in any country, it often affects the markets in all other countries.

That fundamental change in the foundation of what it means to invest in "stocks"— in the basic dynamics of how markets work— has made investing in stock markets more challenging to evaluate reasonably. It has made investing in stock markets more of a gamble, rather than a safe investment. For much of the time sincestock markets came into being, they could be relied upon as a secure investment, as the value of stocks could be depended upon to increase at a rate exceeding other investments. There have obviously been a few major variations in this positive growth, of course, but the overall growth has been something that could be depended on. Because of the connections with markets in the entire world, this security has been destabilized.

On any given day, there is always a good chance that something viewed as "bad" could happen in one country— a country whose economy is a crucial player in the world financial system. There is also a chance that something good could happen. One positive event, however—unless it is extremely dramatic—may not be enough to drive up the value of stocks all over the world. Everything has to be good, everywhere. But one negative event can easily be enough to drive down the value of stocks all over the world.

This dependence on the news by people (investors) who try to predict in which direction the market will go, is, of course, absurd. It is another example of the fact that what we call "value" is actually determined by our individual and group psychology.

If value is determined by how we think, then we should be able to leave our anciently-rooted dependence on external substances to determine value – and the course that our lives take.

A working person may have a 401(k) or an IRA through the person's employer. The money in that account is invested through a brokerage house that buys shares in various stocks on the New York Stock Exchange or other exchanges. A good portion of that investment could be in very large entities that form what is termed the Dow Jones Industrial Average. Let's suppose that one or more of those companies is undertaking activities or investments that cause great damage to the economy of the country, as happened in the 2008 – 2009 economic debacle in the United States.

If you are that person, what will be your perspective on this? You live in a democracy, so your vote helps determine who will be the members of the legislature that decide how to respond. You expect that these financial institutions will pay the price of their own foolishness and intense greed, but you don't want to hurt your own investment in these institutions.

In 2008, instead of paying for the risks they took, some of those institutions were bailed out bythe government. As "punishment", at year-end, high-level executives took their bonuses, as ifthey had just finished a brilliant year.

In this example we see again how the distortion of the system, as well as the definition of "wealth" as "amount of money," can cause destructive behavior in all of us. There are several schools of economic thought that discuss such choices.

The wealth of the United States is currently double what it was only about ten years ago, yet the median household income has remained pretty much the same.

Where is that money?

If you compare our economy to a gambling establishment, the profits went to the "house"—those elites who were in a position to extract the wealth out of the chaos.

Greece, the European Union, and financial institutions

A quick example of the intricacy of our world-wide financial mess was a "crisis" that was being discussed in the news beginning in 2010 and 2011.There was great concern that Greece would default on its debts.

Let's look at how the situation developed. Banks and financial institutions in the United States had lent a great deal of money to Greece; but those honorable institutions had not indicated to the world, especially to the nations of the European Union (of which Greece is a member) that there was anything to worry about. No one knew how much had been loaned to Greece.

Suddenly, the EU came to know that there was, in fact, plenty to worry about. If the government (supposedly representing the people) of Greece defaulted on the loans, then it would throw the entire EU—and by corollary the rest of the developed world—into a deep financial funk.

This would, of course, affect all of you reading this in a much more significant manner than it would affect the bankers at those financial institutions.

So, the other European countries had to loan more money to Greece, and to receive that money the government of Greece was required to change its policies regarding various programs for its own citizens.

But whose money are we dealing with? Who is actually affected? Are we talking about reality, or theory?

How is it that a corporation, in this case a financial institution, is acting as an independent nation-state, but is not subject to any of the hard-world reality—the *risk*— to which a nation-state is subject?

Why does debt to financial institutions differ from debt between nations?

People bought bonds from the government of Greece, and the government of Greece also owed many payments to government employees, pensions of former government employees, etc. Suddenly, Greece didn't have the money to make those payments.

But where did that "money" come from in the first place? Did some supernatural power suddenly materialize a pile of money, but then Greece spent too much? Who said how much money was in the pile?

Although these questions can be answered in terms that have been defined by economists, in reality the answers are abstract and amorphous. We take these concepts for granted, as if they make perfect sense; but in fact, they make sense only within the framework that economists have constructed out of functional necessity. The world did not start out with a certain amount of money, which was structured in certain forms. The people of the world created the money and now dictate what that money represents.

In Spain, a bank had loaned a great deal of money to a soccer (futbol) club to support the club's acquisition of the most famous soccer star in Europe. Later, when Spain's economic situation began to deteriorate and came to be viewed as possibly in need of being rescued by the rest of the European Union, bankers because desperate. At one point, the E.U. contemplated taking possession of the soccer player as security for the debt.

If the idea of a bank representing a coalition of nations "owning" a human being does not strike you as an absurdity beyond normal human thought, then maybe you own a bank.

Every day, major news media organizations, whether on the web, TV, or radio, consult economists to provide comments to help listeners understand the rise or fall of stocks on that day. Shouldn't they be able to tell us what will happen before it happens, rather than tell us what happened afterwards, then giving us the reason?

Events of a few years ago in the U.S. provide an even more striking example of something which the world believes is real— namely, the National Debt, which includes U.S. Savings Bonds. There is almost nothing more abstract. In my view, these notions are even less concrete than the vacuum of space, and perhaps more relevant to us than dark matter or dark energy only because we can actually see them.

When the U.S. Congress failed to structure a meaningful plan to address the nation's debt, one of the institutions that rate the financial status—dependability—of companies, countries and governments, downgraded the financial dependability of the United States.

Soon after this happened the various measures of the value of the stock markets—the various indexes—all showed that the markets had suffered great losses. Institutional investors and individuals had taken their money out of the stock market.

Where did the money go?

A great deal of it was used to purchase United States government bonds.

It's difficult—even in a work such as this, which proposes to analyze the absurdity of the financial engines that drive the world's economies— to discuss such a situation in a serious manner. But let's try.

Because the Congress of the U.S. was unable to address the issue of the nation's debt in a reasonable, thoughtful manner, investors withdrew funds from the U.S. stock market. A great deal of this money was invested in U.S. government bonds. Evidently, people decided that in a period of economic uncertainty the safest thing to do with their money was to loan it to the U.S. government. For anyone not paying attention, that's the same government that was unable to reach a reasonable solution to address its debt crisis, and consequently had its credit worthiness downgraded.

Why did they do this? What is the correlation between a Congress unable to deal with the nation's debt, and the value of stocks? If there were any correlation, wouldn't the bonds issued by that very government have more inherent risk than stock in corporations that function (somewhat) independently of the government?

This brings us back to the idea that the nature of the stock market functioning is a bit like a casino in Las Vegas. The behavior we're talking about was driven by people's psychological fear that the stock market would lose value, not by any action or decision by businesses. Fear caused people's money to flee the market and thus justify people's concerns about the market, creating a self-fulfilling prophecy.

That fear came as a result of the actions of the government of the United States. The government inspired the fear, so people invested their money in that same government, viewing it as the safest place in the world to put their money during uncertain economic times.

Think about what the actions of the credit rating agencies mean. If all monetary systems are dependent upon each other in our global economy, then who is the independent arbiter of any nation's financial situation? A credit rating agency?

Does not the credit rating agency depend for its existence on the structure of the economy of the country in which it exists?

Well, actually, no. It depends more on perception of that economy.

And let us not forget that credit rating agencies are often paid by large financial institutions, so the economic disaster that struck the U.S. in the late 2000's was not predicted by those agencies.

The issue we are discussing is the perception of the "national debt" of the U.S. So, people invested in savings bonds. A savings bond is not actually a "savings," but a loan. When people buy bonds, they are loaning their money to the government of the United States. The government of the United States borrowed their money, increasing the national debt.

This was not only perfectly acceptable to the buyers, but also viewed as a safer investment than stocks, which were devalued because of people's perceptions about the insecurity of the government of the United States—relative to the debt.

"We don't trust the government, so let's give the government our money."

"We don't want the government to owe money, so let's make it owe more money."

Nothing shows the absurdity of the abstract meaning of money more than this strange concept.

6

The Nations

Confidence in the U.S. abounds. If any nation is equipped to comprehend the meaning of wealth and value and money, it is the United States.

People have come to the U.S. from almost every culture in the world, having seen the way each of those cultures function, both politically and economically. The U.S. is the first truly multi-cultural country, and the most truly multi-cultural country in the world. Representatives of almost all cultures and races have come together, sometimes in a more beneficial manner and sometimes in a conflicting manner.

Let's look at the larger questions of financial interactions between nations.

What does it mean when a country loans another country a billion dollars? Or gives that country a billion dollars in financial aid? We again come back to the question of what money "represents"—what it means. When a country gets a billion dollars from another country, what is really happening?

Many countries have a large "national debt." Do we know what that means? One example of a small aspect of a national debt is what was discussed in the previous chapter: the United States issued bonds. The bonds "represent" (there's that word again) a certain amount of money that will be paid to the person who holds the bond at some point in time. The government of China owns a lot of those bonds. So, the U.S. owes China a great deal of money.

This is not the same as your borrowing a few dollars from your neighbor and then paying him back a few days later.

Why not?

The difference is that a myriad of other variables has been introduced into this transaction. When you borrow from your neighbor, that money (the currency, or the numbers) you borrow is "backed" by the government whose money it represents. When a country borrows from another country, who is backing up the money? The term "full faith and credit" is used in such financial transactions. Whose faith? In what? The more we delve into trying to understand these things, the more complex and abstract they become. And if they are that abstract, if what defines every aspect of every financial transaction is our *opinion*, can we not change that opinion?

Dollar bills are not going from one country to the other. Numbers are going from one computer to another. What exactly do those numbers represent? They represent someone's idea that there exists a billion dollars "owned" or possessed by a country. Our ordinary thinking is that if you have a billion dollars in your bank account, you could walk into a store and buy something for a billion dollars. A reminder: That means that a bank is transferring data, or numbers, *representing* a billion dollars from one "account" to another account.

The same thing is happening between countries. The country receiving the money now has a billion dollars it can use to buy food, or weapons. Just think about how abstract this entire transaction is. We're back to our original discussion about what money means, what it represents: This is a *human* concept. Money is a *human* concept. It is not some independent entity, whether it is a transaction between nations or a transaction between companies or a transaction between people. It is not real.

That's the concept that we really have to understand, the concept that is the most difficult to grasp, because it requires us to abandoned something we've taken for granted since we learned that money could buy things; since we, as a species, developed the idea of money: It's the concept that money is not real.

At some moment a long, long time ago, someone picked up a rock and decided that it could represent something else; that is, that rock could be exchanged for something else. And then someone decided that rocks that glittered should be more valuable than other rocks, and could be used to get more things. Whenever that concept began, and whenever the rest of the people began to accept the idea, the question we must ask ourselves is: Why do we still believe it?

A great deal of human activity, of all of our work, all our efforts, the reason we wear ourselves out each day, is to obtain something that's not real. We lose sight of why we are doing all that we do. It's not for the money, it's for what the money can buy; what the money means, what the money stands for. What the money represents.

Coming down to Earth

Land is certainly tangible, unlike money, which is abstract. Yet we have come to live with a perspective that turns that notion on its head. We assign a value to land which is defined monetarily. So, instead of the worth of a dollar being measured in terms of how much land it could purchase, the worth of a piece of land is measured in terms of how many dollars it can capture if sold.

This seems to be a logical development, as societies have emerged from agriculturally based cultures to industrially based, service based, or—as we move forward—information based. We have thus grown to understand that even the most basic, independent determinate of value—land— now has changing value for humans. People live in cities, in accommodations that may be bought or leased, and which have no land at all associated with them.

At one point, the value of everything else was measured by land. But today there is an assumption in all industrially based societies that the value of land is as relative as the value of anything else. It is no longer seen as an objective measurement of value.

In 2011 the United States was trying to recover from a housing crisis; more accurately, from an economic crisis that was partially precipitated when the value of investment instruments related to houses declined sharply and did not regain the previous value quickly. That is, houses were worth less than before. So, anyone who had recently bought

41

a house found that the house was worth less than they paid (including the mortgage, of course); in some cases less than they still owed.

But how can a house lose value? What determines the value— the house, or the dollars?

What is more substantial than real estate? (There is a reason why property is referred to as "real" estate.)

Does value fluctuate based on a house, in terms of how many dollars it can fetch in a sale? Or the dollar, in terms of how it relates to housing? A house is something concrete, but money is something whose value fluctuates.

But somewhere along the way, most of the money began to end up with the development company that organized the whole procedure of constructing a number of houses in a certain area, because they are the people who have learned how to move the numbers (that represent money) in the ways that benefit them the most.

We feel that there must be something constant, something that we can depend upon, so we give value in our perceptions, in our thoughts, to these free-floating abstractions which are as changeable as the wind.

But what can we turn to as an objective measure of value? What is there that can stand independently and offer to us the absolute worth of anything?

Alas, nothing.

PART II

Is Money Working for Us?

"There must be some way out of here," said the joker to the thief

"There's too much confusion, I can't get no relief"

All Along the Watchtower

--Bob *Dylan*

WILLIAM BERNSTEIN

7

Human Lives, or Money?

Do we value human beings, or the "capital" associated with them? Life, or a bank account? We assume that the reason we hold money is so we can live, and ultimately live *better* lives, according to whatever our definition of life quality is.

We shouldn't have to weigh one against the other.

It is exceedingly strange that certain societies, and especially certain segments within societies, view money as more important than human beings. We all know of the most obvious example, one that could not be avoided in our evolution to a money-based society: the actuarial tables relied on by insurance companies. In order to determine whether the company would ultimately lose money or make money on the insurance offered to someone, the company needed to be able to make a reasonable estimate on how long the average number of people—with similar measurable parameters to that individual—would live.

This has been an unavoidable analysis of a person's worth relative to a company's worth, but there is something fundamentally unsettling about the concept. On a lesser scale, what about the countless incidences of companies that denied the existence of problems until forced to acknowledge certain major defects; always with profits in mind? Most major automobile manufacturers have gone through examples of this sort of denial. The most recent extreme example is that of General Motors in 2014 after the company had tried to avoid accepting responsibility for some defects that caused serious injury to some.

In early civilizations, the unquestioned rulers believed it made perfect sense to view humans as objects that existed to benefit the accumulation of wealth for a few. Kings and emperors ruled over laborers in feudal societies, and even enslaved people.

Today, in the 21st century, we believe we have restructured many of those old paradigms that held us back. And yet, the old view of the world has not changed, except in the definitions of who benefits from the "people for money" concept.

Products used to be manufactured with the idea that producing a quality product would lead to more sales of that product. This would benefit the producer of the goods, who would earn more money, as well as those purchasing the goods, who would get a better product.

The progression of the structure of advertising and the confluence of the concepts of advertising along with the revolution in media that took place in the 20th century, especially in the second half of the 20th century, radically changed that paradigm. A structure evolved in which the buying public's *concept* of the product became much more important than the product itself.

What a strange new paradigm this caused! This is another example of the definition of "value" that is being discussed here. In the past, and still today in many cultures, the value of a piece of gold jewelry was determined by the weight of the gold. At least that provides an objective measurement, although as we've postulated here, that measurement is based on the abstract value we have attributed to "money." Is currency worth a certain amount of gold? Or is gold worth a certain amount of money?

The two values are intricately connected, and are interdependent. Is it possible to determine the value of each objectively?

An example of this is that the modern value we place on items such as jewelry is often completely independent of the relationship between that jewelry and the substance from which it is made. The value of a ring made of gold may be determined more by the design of the ring, of who made it, etc. than by the weight of the gold.

This is a natural part of our evolution, but something we should be aware of when we are discussing some basic concepts such as value. So, we have taken a giant step from 1) the society in which an already subjective, abstract value is placed on a substance such as gold to 2) the society in which the value of something is determined by public opinion. And in which that public opinion is influenced by advertising.

Thus, an artificial construct, advertising, becomes a huge industry in which people invest money in order to convince others to spend their money in a certain way.

8

If Resources are Natural, Whose Resources are They?

In the twentieth century, several countries were found to have large quantities of oil.

To whom does that oil belong? To the people of the country?

It doesn't seem to work that way.

Who determines the ownership of a nation's oil?

Whoever is in power at the time.

In certain countries the oil might have represented enough wealth for every person in the country to have had a good life with enough money. But the money went from the oil companies to the people in power, and there it stayed. A few people ended up with huge sums of money, and great wealth.

Certainly, some people have to get the oil from the ground; it has to be managed, and large numbers of people have to be involved at every step of the process of extraction and shipping to a developed country, where it is usually refined and then sold.

What's wrong with this picture?

Sometimes it is easy for us to look at what happens in other places, to other people— but the question we must ask ourselves is this:

Does the same thing happen in our own lives?

Let's take a look at how the "wealth" represented by our natural resources is used.

One of the assumptions we make in today's world is that in order to live, we need electric power. Electricity is produced from various natural resources such as oil, coal, water, and wind. Resources such as natural gas may be used as alternatives to heat our homes. Do we still remember the financial crisis in California that was caused by the manipulation of "energy" prices by certain companies (think Enron)? Is this something that makes sense in the world today?

We must return to the fundamental question of control over the resources, the equipment that transforms those resources into power, and the people who do the work involved. The people doing the work earn money that enables them to live. Like every other transaction, it is ultimately circular.

But somewhere in that circle is a person who controls the movement of the money and takes a cut. And that "cut" has often come to amount to many times the amount that the people actually doing the work receive for their labor.

I'm not saying that the work of the person who controls the money—the manager — is unimportant. I am saying that although systems need oversight and management, systems don't need money. We have used money (in most societies, but not all), since we became civilized, as the means to make things happen. But moving money around as a means for certain entities to accumulate more money is not necessarily a part of the process

Just as the use of money evolved as a means to enable society to function, the control of money has become the overriding force in the structure of our functioning as a society (or as societies).

Let's look at people's relations with this fundamental resource to all economies—oil—in another, very practical way. For the majority of people in the U.S., when the price of oil goes up, they pay more for gasoline, more to ride the bus, more to travel in any manner. But for a very large number of people, when the price of oil goes up, although they have to pay more for gasoline or commercial travel, they may also benefit. These are people who own stock in the oil company.

When the price of oil goes up, if your money is invested in oil stocks, you benefit. On paper, you have more capital, at least for a while. Conversely, when the price of oil goes down, you pay less for gas, but the value of your stocks also may also decrease. And it's actually much more complicated than that: the fluctuations in the price of oil affect the entire economy of any country in significant, complex ways. Affect, in fact, the interactions and economies of every nation, and thus of every person in the world.

If you own some stock in oil companies, but not much, are you better off if the price of oil goes up, or if it goes down? Even if you don't have any investment, what about the effects that rising or falling oil prices will have on the economy of the country in general, and through that overall economy, on you? Are you better off if oil prices go up or down? This example can be extended to every financial transaction, every economic system, all over the world. The very fact that we can ask this question itself seems a bit insane.

There has been a great example of this in recent years. The price of oil had reached unprecedented, extremely high levels. This was a real problem in many ways for many elements of society and for many people. Then the price of oil began to fall precipitously, reaching lower levels than had been seen in many years. This had other negative effects on society and people.

We live in a big economic insane asylum.

Another example of viewing resources as belonging to the people who live in a country is the national park system in the United States. In 1872 the U.S. government declared vast tracts of land as belonging to the people of the country—all of the people—to be maintained by the government; the government is, after all, the people. President Theodore Roosevelt doubled the number of national parks in the early 1900s. This land didn't belong to the wealthiest people, or to giant corporations, but to the public, to everyone. It benefits everyone who has ever been to a national park. If we can do this with national parks, what limits us from expanding our thinking further, other than our own preconceptions?

Of course, the government is also pressured to open precious wild lands to exploitation for economic purposes that will, yet again, unevenly benefit the few individuals pursuing the resources.

New-Age Gold Mines

Precious resources like oil and gold can be mined from the earth, but today, a way has been found to exploit a new resource: your personal data.

In most developed nations, owning a "smart phone" is becoming very common. Soon almost everyone will have smart phones, just as a few years ago almost everyone had land-based phones. We have a lot to think about in our lives, but one thing we don't take the time to think about is the extent to which every aspect of our lives is now a bit of data in some company's data base. Various providers have access to this information, and control over it is still unclear. The definition of privacy has changed significantly. Now we are concerned not with whether someone else knows everything about us, but only if they are hurting us with that information. Whether or not they might hurt us in the future is beyond our mental projections.

Let's look at a perversion of the basic idea being postulated here, that money is basically representative of the value placed on human lives and functioning,

We've been talking about oil, about who benefits from the oil that is under a nation's surface, and the use of that oil compared to other uses of land, such as for national parks. Although some entities are making a tremendous amount of money from the oil that is under our land, they are also given tax breaks. The financial benefits of those tax breaks don't go to the people who work as employees of those companies.

The original reason for tax breaks was to motivate companies to explore for oil so that the necessary fuel would be obtained. But once a company is making an amount of money that dwarfs the income of almost every other company, they shouldn't need much additional incentive to keep making that kind of money.

It's as if I drove a van filled with thousands of hundred-dollar bills to your door and told you, "If you will agree to take this money, I will write you a check for an additional $1,000,000."

And this makes sense to some people.

If you were one of those lucky enough to be in on the deal, you would find a way for it to make sense to you.

In fact, an interesting statistic is that in 2010 the average salary of a full-time, employed person in America went up one-half of one percent (1/2 %). The average CEO salary went up 23%. That was a year toward the end of a serious recession, a year in which economists, politicians, the news media, and the public were talking about how tough the times were. Unemployment was still at a very high level. People were still being laid off. CEOs, as has consistently been the case over the past thirty years, made much more money.

In what way is this capitalism? This is actually the antithesis of capitalism. It is complete control of the economy of the nation—and, to a large extent, the world—in the hands of very few people. It is a new breed of economic system; the closest description we have is plutocracy, control by the wealthy; or oligarchy, control by a small group for their own purposes. Perhaps the best way to describe it would be to call it a "veiled corporate aristocracy." There are kings and queens, barons, earls, dukes, lords and ladies, etc., but they are known by different terminologies, different names that sound so appropriate in today's manipulated world.

"No society can surely be flourishing and happy of which by far the greater part of the numbers are poor and miserable." Adam Smith

9

Life on Earth

In certain nations wildlife preserves have been established to protect endangered species. Most of us would agree that this is a worthwhile endeavor. We would not want those creatures that are still alive in today's world to disappear. And yet animals such as tigers, elephants, and many, many more continue to be endangered by humans.

Hunting in these preserves is illegal; yet, in certain areas the hunting and killing of large numbers of animals continues. The reasons for this are, like everything else, economically based. And that economic basis has, as always, survival as its basis.

When there are not sufficient funds to pay enough people to enforce the laws protecting the sanctuaries, the killing of the animals there increases. And the reason people hunt the animals is, of course, to survive.

So, we must again ask ourselves what value we place on various things. What value we place on a human life, what value we place on an animal life. In today's world, the number of animals who can be killed and eaten in order to feed the human population is limited. Plus, we want those animals. And yet, we don't want people to starve. People are starving and dying of thirst, and the examination we must make is whether we can change this paradigm.

Do we care if people are starving? Do we care if beautiful animals are eliminated from the earth? Should we care?

Do we have a choice?

I believe we do have a choice, and it is not too late to choose in favor of life on earth.

We can choose to create a system in which all people live decent lives with adequate food and medical care, without dramatically downgrading the lifestyles of those who are privileged to have much more than adequate food and care.

Life insurance was created and exists—we assume—to provide for the family of a person who dies. And yet many companies today have what the insurance industry refers to as "dead peasant" policies: Life insurance on their employees.

The employees' families don't collect if the employee dies. The corporation collects.

In today's society we've come to accept this corporate money plan as perfectly acceptable. This is what we have to examine: What is it that has made us immune to questioning this idea that anything involving profit is something natural? This brings us back to the earlier idea of gambling compared to the stock market. This is another form of perfectly accepted, profitable gambling; only this time the bet is on a person's life, and we have been conditioned to not see anything wrong with this.

In 2012 a massive earthquake, measuring 9.0 on the Richter scale, followed by a massive tsunami, struck Japan. 15,894 people were killed, 6,152 were injured, and 2,562 people were missing[four years later. In reporting on the aftermath, many media reports addressed the effects that this unfortunate event may have on the economy of Japan and on the world economy. Although huge numbers of people lost their lives, there was a real focus on money.

The earthquake didn't affect most of humanity personally, so we are free to worry about something else—money.

Here is the reality of life, my friend: Your death will not affect the world economy; but it will affect you and those close to you. Your life has value, independently of anything related to finance, or to possessions.

Yet we continue to measure life in monetary terms.

Another example of the extent to which money has come to dominate people's lives in the United States is the extent to which we have come to structure our children's lives almost from the time they are born. In many families every detail of a child's life is programmed, from the deposit on the elementary school they will attend to the leisure and sports activities in which they will participate.

What's the long-term goal of this obsession with engaging in activities for future advancement, of taking away the natural pace of maturing that a child needs to experience?

The goal of making more money.

Consider the cost of higher education in the United States. The college that one attends is often an extremely important determinant of one's future earning potential. Studies have found that in America, the college choice is determined much more by the amount of money the family has than by the academic history and potential of the student.

Someone with enough money will go to a more prestigious institution of higher learning, which has much greater potential to lead them toward a better career and more earning potential. In recent times this has resulted in a sharp decline in the number of qualified minority students attending college. This statistic is in direct contradiction to our belief that America is a land of opportunity where those who work hard can succeed. It is contrary to the basic principles on which the most of us believe it is founded, and on which we believe it still functions.

10

How do we Value Human Health?

What does the concept of "insurance" mean? We are insuring ourselves against something that might cause serious problems. Let's look at the concept of health insurance, and how something that began as a good idea for both the company providing the insurance and the person being insured has become perverted over the years.

When health insurance first became popular, the idea was to "insure" that people had coverage for their medical expenses. People paid monthly premiums to insurance companies, who in turn used that money to pay for their clients' medical bills. Insurance companies made enough to provide this coverage, and the patients who subscribed to the policies were content.

Things have changed. For many years, we have had a health care crisis in the U.S. The companies that manage insurance, sell policies, and pay insurance claims, have comprehensively transformed their structure. The major focus, the almost single-minded focus, of insurance companies in America today is to make more money, more profit for the stockholders.

In the past, when the focus was on insuring people, the system functioned as it was designed to function. Then the focus shifted from people to money. Today, the funds that provide the major investments in corporations such as insurance companies expect to see a certain margin of profit made by that company. In the past the margin of profit was around 5%. Over time, profit margins became much higher.

It is, however, difficult to determine actual profit margins. The reason it is difficult is linked to the underlining problem we are examining here: numbers are being manipulated and used in varying ways, depending on who is doing the analysis. Outside observers have made it clear that the profit margins today, even after a few years of the Affordable Care Act, are close to 16%.

Consequently, your health is no longer the primary goal. Instead, the goal is to make the maximum profit while paying the minimum benefits. If the profit margin is higher, more stock will be purchased, which will, in turn, cause the value of the stock to increase. And in doing this, the insurance companies have somehow managed to convince many Americans that the fault lies with the doctors who are devoting their lives to treating them, or with the lawyers who might sue medical providers when they make a major mistake and cause serious injury or death to a patient.

We always believe that most of the people who work in the health care industry do so with the hope of helping people get well and stay well. The main concern of those who provide patient care, as well as those who handle the business side of the finances of the hospital, is people's health and well-being.

There is a principle that has operated in some circles that hospitals benefit from flu epidemics, and that cutting those epidemics short or eliminating them would be detrimental to the financial condition of the hospital. If reading that doesn't make you see that there are serious problems in society, that something as insubstantial as money has become more important than human life, you have missed something.

There is a constant danger that the value of investments of stockholders in the for-profit health-care industry will take the place of healing.

Another example of weighing money as more valuable than life is the fact that many important, life-saving drugs are in short supply in the United States. It is costly to manufacture these drugs; so although the final assembly of many drugs takes place in the U.S., the basic ingredients used in these drugs are manufactured in areas where there is little quality control. The money that companies can make—their profit and loss ratio—has become far more important than the final results obtained with the medicine.

Is it not an obvious obscenity that "value"—as measured by money—is weighed against your very life?

A friend of mine is undergoing an experimental cancer treatment that is keeping her alive. For various reasons, although the treatment is working and has continued over quite some time, her specific treatment is not viewed anymore as something that will be paid for by the drug company researching the particular process, so she has to pay an exorbitant amount for each round of chemotherapy.

She has to pay it only if she wants to stay alive, of course. So, her life, and ultimately your life, depends on money. How much is your life worth? This example illustrates why that which we refer to as the free market does not work in all of life's examples, but especially not in health care.

Insurance companies have tables that will tell you how much your life is worth. There are always debates among people who manage to sound quite reasonable (not to me) about how much certain life-extending treatments are worth. If something costs too much, even though it may keep you alive, you're just not worth it.

And, like most issues regarding such health care in the United States, it gets even more absurd. There is a person who, after recovering from cancer, is cancer free. Her doctors detect no sign of cancer; but she still has to undergo the experimental, radical chemotherapy every five weeks. Why?

Because, since the treatment that cured the cancer is experimental, if the cancer were to return later, she could not get the same chemotherapy again. Why not, you may ask. There is no medical, scientific answer to that question, no real need to undergo the treatment every five weeks. The logical idea is that if the cancer returns, she should then get the same treatment. But even though there is currently no trace of cancer, she has to continue that treatment, or else, if the cancer returns, she would not be given the treatment. For the rest of her life. Chemotherapy is not healthy for the human body (or any body). It is a crucial valuable treatment when needed, but the idea of being forced to use it when not needed is a bit of a distortion.

Is this the best we can do? I say we can do better— much better.

Most of the scientists who work in the field of medical research do their work for altruistic reasons: to actually help people, or just for the love of science. They want to earn a living, of course, but they're not the ones making the large amounts of money. The companies that hire them make the big bucks.The companies, of course, put up the investments (the money) to hire the researchers, pay for the experiments, find drugs or treatments that work, and, ultimately, make money.

This makes perfect sense until you think about the larger picture: The medical researchers find the cures, the treatment, the prevention, but someone else makes most of the money.

We've already talked about the fact that they're not actually getting "money" – that is, they're not getting gold, or bills that represent something. They're getting an extremely abstract thing: a number is conveyed from one computer to another showing that an amount is transferred from the company's bank account to their bank account. This amount represents a certain value, something they can use to pay their mortgage or rent, buy food to eat, and other goods. Maybe we can find a better way.

11

Trickle-Down Economics

In the last several decades, the largest corporations have taken the place of feudal lords, and working for the company has taken the place of working on the lord's land. That structure of working for the king could be given the same label as an idea that is believed by many in today's world: "trickle-down economics." The idea underlying this concept is that the corporations or individuals making the most money should be allowed to make as much as possible, as that will benefit those who are at the bottom of the economic ladder. That is, the money will "trickle down" from those with a great deal of wealth to those without much.

Not that many years ago almost all societies functioned in such a system; today we refer to such a structure as a feudal system. The rulers owned the land and everyone worked for them. Those at the bottom of this economic structure were usually told that those at the top were ordained by a higher power to fulfill their roles, and those at the top often insisted they were trying to do everything they could to benefit their subjects (who did the actual work in the kingdom or fiefdom.)

In the latter part of the 18th century and the early 19th century, people in several countries fought revolutions against this concept, and established new systems of government and economics in which ordinary people began to have more power and began to control the way their lives were shaped. But this more "democratic" way of societal functioning often proved difficult to maintain.

The fallacy of the idea that the success and increase in money and power of the wealthiest would benefit others is perhaps best shown in the often-quoted statement by the well-known British historian Lord Acton when he said, "Power tends to corrupt, and absolute power corrupts absolutely."

In the 20th century, as corporations became independent entities and began to find ways to increase their wealth and power, this idea of the wealth "trickling down" to those who were most lacking in wealth began to be adapted by some.

The American Revolution was fought against a system in which the wealthiest continually exploited those who were not so wealthy; but over many, many years, the same system—in a slightly different form and using different names—has been established.

Playing Financial Instruments

It is not work that produces wealth anymore; wealth is produced by manipulation of the money in a system that is structured to be controlled by financial instruments rather than by actual productivity or services.

In the feudal system, the people with all the wealth used their power to generate more wealth, and those without wealth got bare sustenance.

Today, societies are moving toward the same end.

"All for ourselves, and nothing for other people, seems, in every age of the world, to have been the vile maxim of the masters of mankind." *The Wealth of Nations*, Adam Smith

12

Very Legal Gambling

The structure of a system in which people "invest" by giving their money to a company in return for a tiny ownership in that company is a pretty abstract concept. Most of us do not think of ourselves as owning a portion of a company even though we own stock in the company. It's a gamble, although gambling is illegal in many states.

We're putting our money on the table. Imagine a giant roulette wheel, but instead of numbers and colors there are lots of companies. We put our money on the company or companies we think will do the best.

The common perception is that the odds, the potential return on investment, are better at the stock market than they are at the roulette wheel or the craps table. But remember, as we have demonstrated earlier: "The house always wins."

With regard to the stock market, the "house" is not really the stock exchange, which only manages the money; the "house" is represented both by the investment firms that move money around and by corporations in which people invest and to which the money goes. And more and more over the past thirty or forty years, the "house" can be interpreted to stand for the people at the top of the corporations who are taking vast amounts of money—the same money you invest in their company.

If you're one of those people at the top, it's a good game. We see more and more examples of companies in which it doesn't matter how well the company is doing. The people at the top get vast sums of money either way. So, what are they motivated to do? To work at improving the company for the long term— or to make the company look good in the short term, causing the stock to rise and making more for the individuals at the top? Or is even that short-term financial game a motivation, if they know that they will get large bonuses yearly and when they leave the company, regardless of what happens to the company's financial situation?

Let's look at an example of how it is that many of the concepts we take for granted actually destroy our own system in a self-perpetuating, downward spiral. Rather than a spiral, maybe a better analogy would be to compare it to the lemmings' inexorable march to the sea.

Certain retail stores promote themselves as having the lowest prices, but one of the ways they manage to have low prices is by paying employees extremely low wages and forcing the suppliers from whom they purchase products to sell them at rock-bottom prices. As a result, people who work at these stores are barely able to subsist, and certainly cannot contribute much to driving the overall economy of the nation. The companies that have to lower their prices to sell to these stores are continually scraping to keep their costs down to such an extent that the same cycle is maintained within their companies: lower wages, often scrimping on product quality. The only economic system this benefits is that consisting of the stockholders and executives.

In the U.S. between the 1940s and 1973, average wages for employees rose at a faster rate than wages for executives. That began to change, until today the system is so top-heavy that the economic system is unable to function. Buying power for 90% of the population has deteriorated until it is destroying production, at least in the United States.

We have come to value productivity over function; a corporation that produces more with less will achieve greater investment by shareholders, greater "wealth" in the hands of a few people, but less wealth in the workplace, among people in the nation, and in the world.

So, why is productivity something to be treasured above all else?

Estimates are that the World Cup soccer tournament in 2010 cost the world ten billion dollars in productivity; that is the world lost $10 billion because of people's attention to the World Cup. In this example, what does *productivity* mean? If we all worked 24 hours a day, we would produce more. People who own stock in the companies we work for would make more money. Is that what life is about?

And what is viewed as the most important contribution from the people doing most of the work? Productivity. It's the magic word. The stock of the corporation increases, the people at the top make more money, everyone is happy when the productivity of the company increases. Everyone, that is, except the people who are doing most of the work. This is because in today's upside-down world, an increase in productivity often means a decrease in the amount paid out in salaries, either through a reduction in the number of people employed, or in expecting those people to work longer hours.

So, it's not the people doing the actual work who are making more money as a result of working more. Instead it's the people that already have a great deal of money that are capturing more, based upon others' efforts.

Yep, that's the system that we all praise, that we worship because of its fairness.

If a company shows "improved" results, their stock rises. Who benefits?

What if you are an employee who is laid off—fired—in order to show better short-term results, even if the long-term results make the company suffer? The company's stock may see a brief gain as their profit/loss ratio looks good for a while. The long-term effects on the company may be detrimental, but the people who make the decisions to let employees go may not be so concerned with the long-term prospects; especially the people at the very top, who may benefit the most. And the larger macro long-term economic prospects for the economy certainly suffer when more people become unemployed.

"Joe's" father worked for a large company that had a pension plan for its employees; when he retired he had a regular income that didn't depend on market fluctuations. "Joe" has an IRA and can never retire, because his investments never accumulate enough, and the portion he deposits in his bank account never earn enough interest.

13

Surplus or Deficit—Want to trade?

An example of the relativistic perspective with which we view money, finances, and the economy of nations in general can be seen by looking at interpretations of a nation's trade surplus or trade deficit.

If a nation has a trade deficit, it means they are purchasing more products from manufacturers in other countries than they are exporting to other countries, so more money is going out than is coming in. This can be viewed as a bad thing, since the money of the people of that nation is going away; therefore, the nation—its people—are becoming "poorer".

But that scenario actually benefits the people in the sense that they can purchase goods from other nations at a cheaper price. So, it benefits people, but not those companies making the products in their own country; which hurts the people. Is this good or bad?

If, on the other hand, a country has a trade surplus, it means that they are exporting more goods than are coming into the country. This has the converse effect of bringing more money into that nation, which could be looked at as a good thing for the economy overall, yet may be hurting the actual human beings who live in that country, as they may have to pay more for what they buy. But maybe they are earning more, because of the overall benefits to the economy. Whether or not they are actually earning more may depend, of course, on many other factors; so what is viewed as positive or negative from the macro level by international institutions such as the World Bank and International Monetary Fund may or may not be having the same positive or negative effects on the people who live there.

And in the preceding examples we haven't even talked about the effects of the decisions by policy-makers in a nation in determining the "value" of their currency relative to other currencies. We are again weighing the value of human beings against the value of money.

When money happens to tomatoes

A small, simple example of the perversion that we have enforced on our own lives can be seen in something that many people in America buy a lot of: tomatoes. The state of Florida produces a large number of tomatoes. Over the years those tomatoes have been systematically bred to become larger, physically tougher, and more resistant to disease. The reasons for this are obvious: there is more money to be made this way. It's easier and safer to transport the tomatoes; they aren't easily damaged.

It has been, naturally, the giant agri-businesses that have had the resources and motivation to achieve this. Studies have shown that people often choose tomatoes based on what they look like and by the pound, not by what they taste like; tasting tomatoes in the store is generally not an option. So, although one of the results of this process has been to eliminate much of the taste of the tomatoes, there is more money to be made. The companies get paid by the weight of the tomatoes, not by the taste, and the tomatoes are not easily damaged. We are again measuring human lives—human values—against money. In much of our world money is more important than human beings, and thus money trumps values such as taste.

Too big to fail?

Through much of history we have viewed banks as honorable institutions. In the 20th Century, some of the largest U.S. institutions were certain banks that were very well respected.

Then they decided they weren't big enough.

WHAT?

It's a staggering concept, isn't it? The largest banks just weren't big enough. They didn't have a big enough slice of the pie. The justification behind this argument is always, of course, that they were restrained by being allowed to handle only people's money, and that such restrictions prevented them from competing with other institutions. And it would be horrible if anyone should ever, at any time, for any reason, stand in the way of that competition. Competition is, after all, the holy grail of economic life. It's what makes everything better. It's what makes us all have better lives.

Really?

And the same idea is there among the giant corporations in other industries: One company owns another, which owns a third, which owns...

Being bigger ultimately meant making more money, whatever it took. After all, what's the end result of competition? Somebody wins. Winning feels good to anyone. The question is, in order for someone to win, does someone have to lose? Or can we all win? Can we get what we want without "defeating" someone else? This is more than an economic question. It is a basic, human, philosophical question.

14

The New Nation-States

We've been talking about large institutions as some sort of amorphous entities that exist independently of human beings. But humans are using the corporate structure and recognition of that structure by the nations of the earth for their benefit—just as in the past humans used the feudal structure of nation-states for their benefit.

In today's world, large multinational corporations have become the new nation-states. Although some nations may find ways to temporarily control internet content or use of the World Wide Web by their populations, geographical constraints are becoming meaningless in today's world. Corporations are not limited by geographical constraints. They can establish an office in any part of the world that benefits them the most, and operate from there almost with impunity.

The power and control of the world today is through the use of, through the possession of, one thing: money. We delude ourselves into continuing in the belief that land or mineral wealth or armed force controls what happens. All of those are controlled by money. The largest of the world's major corporations are "multinational," operating in many countries and controlling the lives of enough people in the world that nations cannot operate completely independently of these entities.

Economic control is the ultimate control.

Since corporations do not need to control territory militarily, they don't worry about land. If they did need to control territory, they would have no difficulty doing so; they would hire their fellow corporate entities that are in the business of military contracting. The major corporations certainly have enough money to do this, and would then be in control of an army more powerful than most armies maintained by most nations.

There have always been good nations and bad nations. Good nations look out for the best interests of their citizens, and bad nations focus on benefitting those controlling the wealth of the nation.

In the same way, there are corporations that are better or worse stewards of their employees, of their products or services, and of the world.

Does that mean corporations answer to you and me? No, since most stock is held by various investment entities or other corporations.

15

What's It All For?

We all want to be able to lead a good life. We all begin to identify with our employer—that is a natural process. We'll usually defend our employer, even if it is doing things of which we disapprove. And this is certainly not a criticism of most of the people who work for those corporations that may be acting in the best interests of the leaders rather than of the company itself or its customers.

Let's look for a second at the sources of investments in the stock market in the United States. Most people don't spend the time to study individual companies and make investments based on that. Most of us invest in a company that manages our money by picking the stocks in which to invest. Almost all of our retirement accounts, our IRAs or 401Ks, are managed by... that's right, by other large institutions, whose sole purpose is to play around with money. Not even a hint of a product or real service, just the "service" of handling money.

Here's the problem with giving a corporation the same identity, the same power, as a human being: Corporations don't have feelings. They can't empathize. They can't take into consideration all the variables necessary in order to make an informed decision. So those decisions are made with only one thing in mind: the bottom line. That seems to be good for the bottom line, for the shareholders—But maybe not. Maybe that's the short-term view.

Is not the reason we have companies, a stock market, banks, etc. to provide a means for people to live? Is not the reason, ultimately, to have a means for people to live better lives? Let's remember the question we posed early in this book: which is more important: a human being, or money?

If we accept that people are more important than money, then we will remember what money is for: to serve human beings. In fact, it is a means to make their lives easier, more convenient.

Human Progress

There was a time – extremely recently in the history of the earth—when humans lived in caves for shelter. Today, we don't need caves. We've figured out a better way to protect ourselves from the elements. We build structures that are a bit like caves, but much more convenient. There was a time when the only light we could conjure after dark was fire. Today we have harnessed electricity to provide abundant light around the clock. There was a time when the only way we had of recording history was to tell another person a story, and trust the person to pass it on. Then we invented written language. Later, we invented the printing press. And progress continues. Today, many books exist only in electronic form.

Our financial systems have also changed dramatically: for example, from trading shells and beads, to minerals, then coins, paper notes, recently to electronic impulses, and now perhaps to bitcoins, an even more abstract entity.

Despite all the changes, our system is still based on the concept of placing a certain value on that which we call "money," and its exchange for goods and services.

When the automobile first came into general use, many people believed that this new invention was foolish, that it would never replace horses. Today it is the primary means of transportation in most of the world. Change happens.

Change can happen to our basic way of interacting with the world and with other people—or to what we refer to as money—also.

PART III

We Can Do Better

"But you don't see no hearses with luggage racks."

Gimme What You Got

-- Don Henley

WILLIAM BERNSTEIN

16

Alien Invasion

If aliens were to invade the earth tomorrow, they wouldn't need to take over the major nations in the Americas, Europe, Asia, Australia, or Africa. All they would need to do is get control of the financial systems. And those "systems" are rapidly becoming one "system."

Perhaps aliens have already taken over the world's economic system. That might help explain why the emphasis has shifted from human beings to money.

We should probably assume that aliens would be smart enough to realize this, and certainly capable of creating complex financial instruments. They might give them names such as "credit default swaps" and other terms that sound foreign to humans.

But perhaps our better natures should assume that aliens would not be as merciless and inhumane as those of our own species who are driven solely by money.

Perhaps we should work to change the system.

People shouldn't have to suffer the way they do.

Once upon a time, Newtonian physics made perfect sense to astronomers and physicists. That was before Albert

Einstein explained the Special and General Theories of Relativity to us all.

Through our understanding of the Theory of Relativity, we have come to understand that gravity, once viewed as a constant, is dependent on time and space, which are dependent on each other. Animals have understood gravity's effects long before humans applied it in our practical actions in the world. But in the case of financial interaction, our actions in the world have preceded our understanding of the relativity of finance.

Today, our economic system makes perfect sense to those who believe that we are practicing a true capitalist model. But this system has been perverted, and is in any case outdated.

It's time for an updated theory.

Do we need economic systems?

One point that needs to be addressed is the idea that anyone questioning the way our economic system operates must be attacking capitalism. People in the United States often fear that any criticism of capitalism leads to some sort of socialism or communism, often for some reason equated with their opposite, fascism.

We are told that Western societies, especially the U.S., are based on the capitalist model.

The reality that we must begin to understand is that the economic system operating today in the United States of America is a far cry from the capitalism that our nation's founders believed in, which was based to some extent on the philosophy expressed in the seminal work on that economic system, *The Wealth of Nations.*

The modern economic model driving the United States has been driven by manipulative greed, which is not identified as such even by those perpetrating it, and has become like the nuclear reaction that powers the sun: feeding on its own energy.

The sun may last billions of years, but this system cannot.

Money exists as a representation of human productivity (supply) and conversely, human desires (demand). Money has come to be viewed as worthy in an independent sense, apart from that which it was created to represent. Historically, the financial sector of any economy has always existed to support the other sectors such as manufacturing and services. A slow, inexorable shift has occurred, until the financial sector has become the engine on which much of the rest of the economic system depends.

This is a self-perpetuating, meaningless system. In this system, the creation of wealth becomes the sole object; determined by, and dependent upon – the creation of wealth.

But money, or what it represents, is not a self-sustaining concept. It is abstract, a representation of something, a means to power the system that provides human beings with their needs and wants.

Let's return to our inherent ingenuity as *homo sapiens* and ask ourselves: "Is this the best we can do?" There are some important reasons that compel us to ask ourselves that question.

A human life should not be valued in the same way as items used to support that life. Economic Darwinism is not necessary in today's world.

Consider the fact that we have enough resources to support the earth's population.

Technology in agriculture has advanced to the extent that the great majority of people in the industrial world no longer have to work in farming in order to feed themselves and the rest of society. In the same way, other industries have been reshaped, and continue to be reshaped, to the extent that there are enough products of all types being produced in today's world to enable every person on earth to lead a comfortable life.

According to some recent studies, the United States of America produces twice as much food as it needs each year. There are about 300,000,000 people in the US, so that's enough food to feed a lot of people. The population of Australia is about 22,000,000; the country produces enough food to feed another forty million people, according to the Australian Federal Agriculture Minister in October, 2011.

In this treatise, we're not talking about the creation of wealth or the means to redistribute wealth. We're postulating the idea that we don't need wealth. Wealth is an outdated concept.

What is money worth in terms of human life?

Ultimately, money should make it possible to live, and make it easier to live, and make our social processes easier. In modern times it is obscene that people die due to a calculation of what it would "cost" to keep that person alive. Actuarial tables analyze data to estimate the probability and likely cost of an event such as death, sickness, injury, disability. Value is defined in terms of dollars; so, we must all ask ourselves the questions: Is not the very concept of "value", the foundation of its meaning, based on human life? Should not value be determined in terms of something's relevance to humans?

To look at money, an intangible concept that exists in order to facilitate our lives, as having an intrinsic value of its own, independent of itself is so absurd that it is difficult to understand how that belief became so prominent. People are important. Life is important. Financial systems exist to serve people.

Most of us tend to assume that before money, many cultures used a "barter" system, in which an item would have been exchanged for another of equal value. For example, I trade you four apples for a piece of clothing. It is believed, however, that many older civilizations operated without either money or a barter system; that is, you would give something to another person in your group with the assumption that when you needed something, someone would give it to you.

Pacific Island societies prior to the nineteenth century were essentially gift economies. This practice still endures in parts of the Pacific. There are several small societies existing today that practice this economic system. These are various islands where basic needs are shared, and things of value are exchanged as gifts, in a reciprocal manner, between people.

Such simplistic ideas seem too primitive to us as we move in our highly structured, systematic, precisely-defined world, where every path has a sharp corner with a name. But the real world in which we live wasn't drawn by a computer, wasn't drawn in squares and triangles. The world is a much more malleable place, consisting of curving concepts and bending lines. The type of economic system in which people give to each other is much more in consonance with our basic nature.

The reason such economies are viewed as insignificant by most in the "developed" world is based on power. Societies that have produced better weapons, that based success on defeating others, have come to control most of the world. If you control more, you are viewed as better.

Anthropologists hypothesize that in ancient cultures an abundance of what was needed to live naturally lead to an economy of giving and sharing, since there was enough for all.

Ironically, the modern world is poised to enter an "economy of abundance" on a much greater scale. There will be enough for everyone, but everyone does not have enough. The United States produces enough food to feed double its own population, and Australia could feed more than double. The means of distribution are also at our fingertips. Yet much of the world goes hungry. Why?

This is, of course, because of the distortion of some of the most basic human qualities—qualities that lead us, originally, to socialize and function as a group. Recent scientific theory holds that the human species, culture, and humanity advanced because of cooperation rather than competition. Humans are social animals. It was our socialization that enabled us to evolve into what we are today, that separated us from other species. Not competition, but socialization.

Yet as we evolved, developing first an agrarian society, in which we did not have to spend all our days hunting, and then developing industries which brought people together into cites, more and more appealing things presented themselves to those who saw that they could take advantage of the new, developing social and economic systems, to "possess" those things.

All economic theories are based on the assumption that some representation of worth, of value, is needed in order to function as a society that enables people to interact with each other, that enables groups to interact with each other, that enables societies to interact with each other. The principles set forth by philosophers of economic theory such as Adam Smith and Karl Marx, who expressed such diverse views, as well as modifications of those and other theories, are all based on certain assumptions that have evolved from the time humans became an agriculturally based society.

Humanity has changed. Our species has changed, and is changing at an exponential rate. We can now afford to challenge our previous assumptions. As people we have evolved into cultures with new paradigms that enable us to function without the rigid structures that have caused such disparity in all of life's conditions.

The question we should be asking ourselves is: Can we live without money?

Can we progress as a society or as a group of societies, as a country or as a group of countries, as a people or as a species, to manage the whole thing in a better way?

We are on the verge of a technology that enables us to live inside virtual worlds. Today's video games move when we move, and we identify with that which we see on the screen. That identification is becoming so real that we are able to "step into" the world created by the game—and by the form of entertainment in which we are participating—to such an extent that we will experience visual, auditory, and other sensory experiences similar to what we experience in our "real" world lives. We will feel that we are inside the game; it will feel real.

Is the money there real?

Is the money in current games—the games we play in our everyday lives—real?

Eventually aspects of our own mental functioning might be downloaded to computer chips. In that case, are we still real?

The money in those virtual worlds is as real as the money in the world in which we move every day.

Before computer games, we played physical board games – Monopoly, for example. Let's apply the same standards here that we apply to Monopoly money. Once we enter that virtual world, the computer generated, virtual world money will seem as real to us as the money we visualize having every day. We're creating our idea of what money is— here in our world—in the same way we create money in the virtual world. It is no more real than that.

We're making it up.

It's probable that the main reason that our species survived, as opposed to Neanderthals, was that we were more successful at cooperating, at working together to overcome the many dangers that could have eliminated us. At some point we began to plant and cultivate crops. This was the true beginning of civilization. The competition between us and other mammals, birds, and fish was not involved in this agricultural cooperation. It wasn't by being more successful at competing and killing that we became the dominant species, but rather by cooperating and sharing.

Yet at each step of the way, in certain societies, we formed groups to compete with other groups. At some point the idea came that land was "property"; that someone should own the land that had belonged to all. Over time that ownership became more and more structured; one person owned more and more land, generally by fighting the person who owned the nearby land. Then these parcels of land coalesced into larger and larger areas, until categories of ownership developed.

In most of the world we gave those who controlled large portions of land titles, and they would portion out parts of the land to other people to control: the owner of the most land was the "king" or "queen"; those who owned smaller portions within the monarch's land area were "earls", "barons", "dukes", and so on. And the kings, barons, and squires who controlled the large portions of land wanted their children to keep the land. So, the claim on the title, and therefore the land, was inherited.

Wealth was determined by how much land someone owned or controlled. Here again we are talking about the concepts of wealth, value, and money. The land had value because it produced food, so at least there was a distinct, immediate connection between the idea of value of land and that which it represented: the ability to keep people alive. But the concept of "ownership"—the idea that one person (or group of people, such as a family) somehow possessed the land—remained a completely abstract concept, attributing a certain *value* to the land and to the person who owned the land.

There were societies where this artificial concept of exclusionary ownership was not practiced, societies where the land was shared. Some of these societies evidently lived in a state of peace, a state in which members of the society lived in a harmonious, sharing culture. Even among those groups, of course, there was often fighting with other groups

Many have interpreted the rise to power of the more competitive societies as part of the natural evolution of humanity. Many of the Europeans who extended their reach around the world over several hundred years believed in the concept of "manifest destiny". Manifest destiny was a religious concept, of course, as distinguished from an evolutionary concept, yet the two are used often enough as the foundations for similar perspectives that it is not a stretch for us to use the terms in a similar fashion.

Interestingly enough, many who believed, and who still believe, in the idea of evolution economically (although not using the term "evolution") reject the concept of evolution of a species, while applying the concept to political and economic structures. This was discussed in Part II: the idea that those who get the most, who manage to accumulate the most "wealth," even if that happens through lucky breaks, *deserve* to have the most. It is based on a similar way of thinking as manifest destiny.

We have seen, however, that some of the most important evolutionary advances came as we cooperated, rather than when we fought.

Human civilization has evolved to the point that the most real, concrete, substantial entity we can conceive, land itself, is often perceived by us as an abstract entity. Its value is measured in terms of something else that has only

93

representative value: money. It is a number on an account sheet somewhere; and perhaps that "somewhere" exists only in cyberspace.

Now that we realize just how ephemeral and insubstantial all of these representative values are, it is time for us to move on. We can develop healthier, more productive ways of functioning as a species, a species that is now interconnected in ways that no one could have imagined even a hundred years ago.

17

American Values

The United States of America was founded on some revolutionary ideas.

The idea that all people are created equal.

The idea that all are endowed "with certain inalienable rights," such as "life, liberty, and the pursuit of happiness."

The nation stands for this concept: Equality. This remarkable, revolutionary perspective that the founders of America incorporated as the basis for the society, evolved over time to approach a more and more accurate equality. But what has also been created over time, what many believed was a new world order, has also been distorted. America could begin carrying through with the ideas that are its foundation, the ideas that promote true equality, by working on structuring a world in which there is true economic equality.

The Golden Calf

This treatise is proposing the idea that we have stepped beyond the necessity of having to represent something— something of value—with something else. We no longer need to identify food, or a house, or a car, as being worth a certain amount of money. We've talked about money being a tool for humans to use to make their lives easier, but money is—has always been, and will always be—a tool that can be used by humans to make their lives easier. If it is manipulated to make people's lives harder, then it has lost its value as such a tool.

So, the very term *value* has to be interpreted in a different manner than that to which we are accustomed. Let's stick to the meaning of value in terms of benefit for human beings, rather than demeaning it to interpret it as directly relating only to the accumulation of things; that is, the accumulation of what we identify as money or wealth.

Let's restate that last sentence: "value" is a measure of the extent to which something is of benefit to us. Even if we interpret the word as it relates to monetary worth, that worth is still measured, ultimately, in terms of benefit to people. We seem to have forgotten that principle somewhere along the way. For some reason it seems that it's easy for people to forget the things that are the most important.

It takes many people to build a house. The electrician who wires everything needs to earn money so that he can buy groceries. He buys groceries at a store, and that money goes to the people who work at the store, to the farmer (not really to a farmer anymore, but more often to a giant farming conglomerate that controls their industry), to the people who drive the trucks that deliver the food to the store, and so on.

Those people are, in turn, all buying groceries and paying a mortgage or rent. Banks loan money to help finance the grocery stores and the mortgages. The bankers go to doctors when they're ill or for physicals, just as the electrician who wired the house does. The doctor uses the money he gets from the banker or the electrician to buy groceries and pay the mortgage or the rent.

The doctor is, of course, actually getting paid by an insurance company, who takes money from the banker, the electrician, etc. and pays the doctor for the work; the insurance company is just another entity through which the money can circulate. People sell insurance, and themselves buy groceries, pay rent or a mortgage, and go to doctors.

There are two basic questions that are obvious, that jump out at us from the idea that we can fundamentally change that way of functioning, and one immediate objection:

1) Could we really accommodate all these people with houses? With food?
2) Would the doctor get the same kind of house as the electrician?
3) These concepts sound like what was tried under the Communist governments in the Soviet Union, and nobody got anything nice there, and in the long run it didn't work.

The answer to number one is that with the advances in modern agriculture, there can be enough food, even good food, to serve everyone. There may be some obstacles in the system, but there is plenty of food. There's plenty of everything, in fact.

The second question is the more difficult question, the question that makes us run away from considering the whole issue of what it means to have money. That is, the question of what money means. The question of the meaning of money.

Wait—Surely no one would work hard to be a doctor if they didn't get a lot more than other people get for doing what they do. In fact, no one would work at all if they could get what they want without working—isn't that right? We think, it must be competition is what motivates people to do more, to keep achieving better things.

In the Biblical story of Exodus, when Moses is away from the people he is leading for some time, they create a golden calf to worship. When he saw that, Moses threw it in the fire and melted it. Maybe we can begin to react in the same way to the concept in the previous paragraph.

18

Relativity and Humanity

Albert Einstein didn't produce The Special Theory of Relativity and The General Theory of Relativity to make more money than his neighbor. Jonas Salk didn't discover the vaccine for polio to make more money than his cousin. Neil Armstrong didn't go to the moon to make more money than his doctor. The police officer or fire fighter didn't go into that occupation to make more money than the corporate executive.

Money is often the motivation for people to begin doing the work that they do. But once they have been doing that work for some time, most people are driven to do what they are doing by other forces. They develop skills at what they do that they are proud of. People depend on them. They begin to take pride in their work.

As a people, as a species, are we ready and able to step beyond the structures that were originally needed, but now only impose limitations that prevent all of us from having the lives that we could be having?

What we're talking about here is not an economic system at all. It's a human system that transcends economic concepts. So far everything in most economic systems is based on competition, but we must ask ourselves some fundamental questions about some of our assumptions about competition: Do better doctors make more money? Or do doctors who promote themselves better and take up the latest trends make more money? What defines "better"? Do the doctors who save more lives make more money? What determines who does?

In a New Yorker article, Atul Gawande points out that general practitioners improveoverall outcomes, but they make much less money than specialists. http://www.newyorker.com/magazine/2017/01/23/the-heroism-of-incremental-care

Do the best products generate the most return (the most money)? A little earlier we discussed how advertising often determines the demand, the "value" of products.

In the communist systems that existed in the Soviet Union and elsewhere, there was no provision for a good life for everyone. The system, like any economic system, was perverted by those who had more power. Those people got more things, had a better life, and the great mass of people who weren't at the top of the system had a tough time.

Everything is relative.

In the U.S. the majority of the people have a decent life with better goods—better houses, better food, more entertainment—than the majority of people in the Soviet economy had. Yet, today many people would say: "The system, like any economic system, was perverted by those who had more power. Those people got more things, had a better life, and the great mass of people who weren't at the top of the system had a tough time."

The most obscene statistic today in the U.S. is that the wealthiest 1% of the population in America has 90% of the wealth.

We don't need to redistribute wealth; we need to eliminate the need for wealth.

Why do people seek great wealth? Bigger houses, more land, fancier toys, better food... basically, things that make us feel good, that enable us to enjoy ourselves more.

Would the electrician be motivated to do the wiring in a house, or in houses, if there were no specific payment for doing it, but if he were able to live a good life? What is his definition of a "good life"? Can that electrician get the life that he or she desires? Would the police officer or the fire fighter still work to protect and save people if they didn't get paid specific amounts, but could live the life they desired? What about the doctor?

What about you?

If we had the option, many of us might like to be able to spend more time enjoying ourselves than time we spend working, but we would still choose to continue the work that we do. The world would continue. Medical researchers would continue to seek cures and vaccines. People would continue to build houses, to cook meals, to run telephone systems.

Is what I just said true? Would people continue to work? Perhaps most importantly, the question we might naturally

101

ask is: Would humanity continue to advance? Would innovations continue? Would people make the hard efforts required to invent new things?

We assume that the driving force behind much of what takes place in the world today is the desire to make money. Is the desire really for the money, or is it for that which the money brings? Obviously, it's for what the money brings, what the money *represents*. It represents more stuff, it represents enjoyment, it represents being able to do what you want.

Can you achieve those things without the money? Can humanity, people the world over, have a good life without the drive for money?

Because of the way in which the economic systems of the entire world have been and are structured, a relatively small number of people benefit from the fact that we use a representative system, in which money represents some arbitrary value, and must be the means by which people get what they need; money is the means by which they attain their goals.

All economic systems share this foundation, whether capitalist, socialist, communist, or other variations. The barter systems practiced in many ancient societies (and a few remotes ones today) didn't have a structure in which the accumulation of money or its equivalent enabled a small number of people to take advantage of many others— but there were other means through which this dominance occurred, such as accumulation of land and feudalism.

We all need food, and we want good food, interesting food. Although we know that many people in the world, and even in our country, don't have enough to eat and would be satisfied with merely having enough to eat, those who have more in today's world wouldn't be happy with a simple meal of rice and beans. Although we know that many people in the world, and even in our own country, don't have a decent roof over their heads, those who have more wouldn't be happy with a simple cabin.

But the reality of the world today is that no one should have to settle for the minimum. When we hear the expression, "there's enough to go around," or "there's enough for everyone," that doesn't mean we should have to settle for less so that someone else can have enough. There is a plethora of material, of food, of services, of people to provide all of these to each other.

Throughout the years of human civilization, many have had the dream that people could all live some sort of utopian life by sharing everything. These dreams have always been just that, and only that: dreams. The very word "utopia" has come to have negative connotations; as if the structure of a society in which everyone has what they need to live a healthy life is a bad thing. Ask yourself: Is this not a distortion of our basic desires as human beings?

A simple example of the changes that society sees due to changes in learning or technology or desire to maximize profit can be seen at the place where you go to get gasoline for your automobile. Not too long ago, every gas station in the U.S. employed attendants who put the gas in the car, checked the oil, took a look at the engine, checked the tire pressure, and washed the windshield. Today that type of organization is rarely seen, except in a few states where, by law, the system cannot be changed.

Another example is the self-checkout counters that have appeared in most major grocery store chains.

In both of these examples, many people are no longer employed by the companies that previously paid them to fill your car with gas or to add the total of the groceries you bought and then accept your payment. Before too long, when you buy something at the supermarket, your cell phone will scan the price and automatically deduct it from your bank account.

A well-accepted theory is that the people employed in these and other industries that are declining and eliminating employees can, and must, find work elsewhere; these former employees can be retrained to do other work that is more suited to our changing times. But as our technology continues to change, as machines continue to be driven by smaller and smaller chips implanted in them, the human beings that did that work previously become less and less crucial to the continued operation.

Where will taxis (or Uber) be when a driverless car can take you where you want to go? Perhaps a more relevant question is, "Where will the drivers be?

These changes are going to happen. Fewer people are going to be employed; the model that has carried the human race through the last many years, with each change leading to new industries and services in which people can be employed, is no longer a dependable model. There will continue to be more people with less opportunity.

The structure of everything we do can, must, and will change. We have no choice but to recognize this change and develop a new structure for the manner in which society operates, the manner in which people's lives are supported and maintained.

We are able to transfer the numbers from your bank account to another bank account—that is, to the bank account of the company that produces the food you bought at the store, or the gas you put in your car. And what is transferred? Only a number.

That transaction seems to many of us almost as abstract as the extent to which we understand the reality that time is relative to velocity, or that energy equals mass times the speed of light squared ($E=MC^2$). Yet, although most of us admit to some lack in our grasp of relativity, we think we understand what is happening to our money.

One simple, concrete example of this might be what we experience in our negotiations to purchase a car. Concepts relating to interest charges, the "cost" to the dealer, the car company's policies, etc. are thrown at us in a cascade of confusing numbers. It can be confusing and overwhelming to the most knowledgeable among us.

It is not a very great leap, therefore, to assume that this whole transaction should be able to occur without the physical representation of whatever it is that we assume is represented by the corresponding "money." Considering how far we've come and how fast change happens in today's world, we can find a way to function as a society, as societies, as the world—without depending upon a unit of measurement that has become so abstract as to make the determination of its value completely arbitrary, to the point that it has lost its true meaning.

The evolution of the current financial system—in which an arbitrary "something" is used to determine the "value" of everything in the lives of all people—was necessary to bring humanity to where it is today. But today that system harms more people than it helps. Is that not a flashing, glaring warning sign that it's time for a change?

Human culture has advanced through things that have increased our ability to cooperate, rather than those that enabled us to compete. The printing press and the computer created tremendous leaps for humanity. Competitive inventions, such as the crossbow or the machine gun, have enabled the society that was first in possession of them to succeed over other societies, benefitting some people briefly, but it has always been the things that bind us together that advanced humanity the most.

The ingenuity of humans that has advanced the human race over time has not been motivated by competition or money, but by the inner drive that we have as a species. An example of this is a mother's love. Mother's love is what introduces us to this world. It is not based on competition or destruction, but on cooperation.

Most of us believe that humans are, at heart, good. Humans have an inherent desire to do the "right" thing. What if we decided to do only what was good, what was right? This is not unnecessarily complicated: we all have a pretty good feel for what is right, for what is good (most of us do, anyway; there are some exceptions that are often based on brain structure). It's part of our basic nature as human beings, part of how we've evolved. The mores that we have established for ourselves feel very natural because they have worked to preserve us for thousands of years.

There have been many societies over the course of human history that functioned based on principles of cooperation, sharing, and caring. Because they were not competition-driven, they didn't focus their energy on producing the most efficient weapon, but rather on taking care of their fellow humans.

The fact that many of these societies no longer exist, were conquered, or otherwise disappeared does not provide an argument for more aggressive culture. The theory of relativity did not spring from Einstein's brain as a means of conquering an enemy, or in order to make money. The printing press was not created as a tool of war.

19

Where do We Go from Here?

Let's look farther back and take a more significant, far-reaching leap in our history: the transition from a hunter-gatherer society to an agricultural society. Growing crops was a cooperative endeavor, and more cooperation meant more food for everyone. People first lived on the land, rather than owning the land.

But we never left our hunter-gatherer ethos. That is why power and control became a fundamental part of certain cultures.

We are, realistically, at the point in our evolution as a species that can enable us to transcend some of the atavistic notions that have directed our lives over thousands of years. We've come to live in a world in which we can realistically say that everyone in the world can and should have good living arrangements, good food, good water, good medicine.

We believe that people are basically good; that it is most often circumstance, driven by the absence of money—or rather, by the absence of what that money can buy—that drives people to do things that are dishonorable, untrustworthy, disreputable, etc. Babies don't start robbing banks or shooting people. They learn to do those things. What if they didn't need to do those things?

There will always, of course, be those who take advantage of any system, who are driven to abuse and mistreat others for their own gain. Today many of those people are either in jail, at risk of going to jail— or they are running major institutions (with virtually no risk of going to jail.)

As a society, we have always found methods of dealing with those who abuse others, and we will continue to find ways to handle those who disturb the order of society in negative ways and harm others. But that should not impede our efforts to build the world that we are able to build, the world we have dreamed of but thought was impossible. Just as many individuals throughout history have achieved things long viewed as impossible, we can achieve such impossibilities as a people, as a race.

People are guided by a sense of what is right, what is fair. It's fundamental to our structure, a basic part of what makes us human. All societies are structured in accordance with that sense of what is right, what is just. Each aspect of any culture is based on that determination, although it may be defined differently in each culture. The definitions may be determined by a religious basis or by that place where the power in the culture is based, but the guiding principles are always based on what is fair, and what is just.

"Economics" is no different than all other bases that regulate the functioning of societies. People have tried to construct the system based on their perception of what is in their best interests. But in a culture where the power (which is today defined by money) is in the hands of a few people, it is determined by what is just or fair for them. In a democracy we assume that the system is constructed in a way that is in the best interest of as many as possible, rather than a few.

I began with a discussion of the meaning of words such as "value," rather than talking about economics, which we have discussed as being entirely too artificial. Let's dare to ask: Why do we need this economic system? I will grant that we used to need it, as we evolved as a species, to help structure civilization. But today it is outdated, and is not serving us well.

Let us make a giant leap of logic, a leap of faith in the goodness of humans, a belief that we can overcome the petty squabbles over land and beliefs that prevent us from moving forward. Certainly, such disputes between societies and peoples are not going to end overnight; but thatshouldn't stop us from brainstorming. Let us apply our highly developed mental abilities to see what potential lies ahead for us once we are able to overcome these obstacles to our advancement.

Let's imagine where we have been and where we're going; where our parents and their parents were, and where our children and their children will be; and more than that, let us think about where they *can* be.

Do we need a piece of paper to represent ownership of a certain amount of wealth?

Can we motivate a person to build houses, to learn the medical science needed to cure disease, to teach children, to grow food, and to do the other countless things that make life possible without "paying" that person in something representing a certain "value": something we call "money"?

The transactions that are involved in every aspect of the life that we live as members of industrial societies take a great deal for granted and are remarkably intricately structured. Take the example given earlier of the person working to build a house. The labor of many people is required. There are those who cut down the trees, who bring the trees to be cut into usable lumber, who work to shape the lumber, who get the products used to make the cement, who dig the hole for the foundation, who pour the cement, who make bricks, who use bricks or wood to make the walls—this list could go on for a long, long time.

We've already established that the "payment" is a completely abstract concept, based on our belief that the "money" that one person is giving to another person "represents" a certain "value." We arbitrarily assign a monetary value to the building materials; let's say bricks.

Do we really need to go through all these steps? All that's happening is that "wealth" or "value" is being transferred, from one person to another. We make that transfer remarkably more complex than it needs to be, so that the numbers that represent money move from one place to another. From the account of the person who will live in the house to the account of the company that hires the builders who hires the people to build the house to the account of the person who lays the bricks to build the wall and to the account of the person who makes the bricks, and so on.

Some people grow up desiring to be doctors and have the ability to pursue the learning required to practice that profession. Some people grow up desiring to build houses and have the ability to learn to do that. People are motivated by different factors. And people will do the things that feel good to them, even once we develop our ability to make all these things happen without the intermediary of having to use such an artificial construct—money—as a means of functioning. And there is no turning back from a society in which computers and artificial intelligence do most of that work. Individual learning of new skills will not solve the challenges that arise from this paradigm shift. Societal learning is required.

The transformation from the industrial society to an information society began long ago. Money is part of the various societies that have gradually evolved as we learned and developed. Does it still have a place here?

Just as space exists relative to time and motion and gravity, and time exists relative to space and motion and gravity, everything on which we place a certain "value" is relative to everything else. Only in this case, it is the human mind that determines that value.

We built our own cage and have been content to lie in it for thousands of years. It is time to allow our minds to transcend this cage by understanding relativity as it applies to our lives.

Making the leap out of our pre-conceived notions is a challenge. We think we have some understanding of what it means to view the universe as it is defined by relativity, but we still tend to think in Newtonian terms. We see everything as existing in an objective, independent manner, rather than the reality that everything exists in a subjective, interdependent, relative manner. We know, for example, that if someone is traveling in a spaceship at extreme speeds, that person might return to earth after twenty of their years had passed, but a hundred years had passed for those on earth. But relating to this sort of understanding—that is, truly understanding—is very different than reading it or even having a mental concept of the theory. And this sort of example is simpler and easier to grasp than some principles of quantum mechanics. And can we really understand that light is both a wave and a particle, depending on how it is viewed?

Our minds face similar constraints as we struggle to understand the remarkably artificial constructs we have used to define financial structures and functioning. The human mind does not easily comprehend the idea that this "value" is under our control. We tend to think in terms of structures that are constant and can be measured independently.

The time has come for us to change our thinking about money and what it represents, just as the Theories of Relativity and Quantum Mechanics ask us to change our thinking about our concepts of the physical universe.

We are close to reaching the point in our development where, without this intermediary, without money, the world

113

will continue to function. People will continue to get not only what they need, but also what they want. We are not far away from that day.

All that's needed is for enough people to realize that the way to the next level of functioning is for nations, for populations, for the people of those nations, to start thinking in a new way.

This change in perception has taken place innumerable times throughout human history. What we now call "city states" merged (often by force) into much larger entities that were eventually called nations. Those nations brought together the various peoples, including languages, currency, and culture, of the various groups that previously existed separately and independently. For this to happen, usually some catastrophic event was required, such as one entity conquering another by force; but occasionally it happened by mutual agreement.

Such change is happening in the world today, not through military force, but through communication. From the time of the printing press, which enabled the writings of one person or group to be much more easily obtained by large numbers of people, significant transformations occurred in the methods of communication between people. These transformations began increasing at an exponential rate with the coming of the telegraph, the telephone, radio and then television.

Then home computers became more common, at the same time that the internet was born and became the most inclusionary structure in human history. The internet, personal computers and cell phones have brought an exponentially rapid leap to a communication that is beyond anything that could be imagined just a few years ago.

Although there remain many places in the world where large numbers of people don't have drinking water, much less access to electricity and computers, theoretically it is possible for anyone, anywhere in the world, to be instantly connected to anyone else, anywhere in the world.

That which prevents this connectivity, as well as the access to electricity and, more importantly, potable drinking water, are those same numbers about which we've been talking—those numbers that represent money, something that we've already established is an artificial concept, an imaginary entity. An imaginary entity is keeping people from having something very real, something extremely substantial: water that they can drink to stay alive or enough food to eat.

The world is not short of resources. There is enough food, enough water, for the earth's population.

Now let's continue to focus on the connectivity of the world. Let's focus on the connections that the billions of people who live all over the world have with each other. Those connections have already started to create significant political change in parts of the world, places where no one imagined that such dramatic restructuring of political systems could take place.

Suddenly it is possible for hundreds, thousands, millions of people to talk to each other instantly, without any intermediary.

One of the largest intermediaries that is functioning in human life is money. Money stands as something that is at once a conduit and a universal impediment to human movement, advancement, transformation.

The internet has bypassed all of the walls, all of the impediments that previously delayed communications between people. People all over the world are beginning to realize that they are more alike than they had imagined; that they all want the same things. And they are starting to realize that that there are certain impediments standing in the way of their obtaining those things.

But more importantly, they are realizing that they can overcome those impediments.

One of the arguments that has always been used by those opposing any change to the economic systems most in use in today's world, that is at the core of almost all of today's major economies, is the principle that assumes that ambition, assertiveness, and motivation are at the heart of any successful major world economy.

The first point in response to that argument is that what is being outlined in this treatise is not an economic system. It is the suggestion that an economic system should no longer be needed in the world that is being created, the world to which we are all evolving and moving.

The next point is that people who are driven, who are ambitious, will continue to be ambitious and driven, and will thus continue to do things to promote the advancement of humanity. Likewise, those who are driven to take shortcuts by abusing others as their means of achievement will continue to pursue the negative side of human activity. Limiting the scope and the opportunities to take devious and hurtful advantage of others is always a useful and worthy course to take, and is the course that has—with many bumps along the way—led the human race in our continuing move toward better living conditions. These better living conditions include better health, better shelter, better communications and, hopefully, a better understanding and empathy toward our fellow human beings.

As difficult as the implementation of a transformative mode of human interaction would be, it would only require the agreement of the world's major financial powers. If the major players decide that they are going to operate in a way that benefits all; the rest of the world will go along, just as the world has always operated in accordance with the financial structure of the strongest nations. That will, of course, change as the old system is dismantled and the people of the world are empowered to function in a new, cooperative manner in which the very concept of "value" and "worth" are redirected.

We haven't talked about people and groups of people who want to harm others for reasons not related to possessions, but for other reasons, such as religion or tribalism. What is being discussed here will not change those ancient tendencies; the only change will be in the system used to operate such antagonism. Hatred and antagonism are based on many factors, and although people who want to fight others because of perceived differences in race, religion, and ethnicity may or may not be encouraged or discouraged by differing value structures, it is also true that the hatred often fueled by those perceptions of other people's differences might be ameliorated by greater means of communication and opportunity, and greater fairness in sharing resources. Maybe not, but there's always hope.

20

Our Own Equation

Since we know that money is a complete abstraction to which we assign a representational value, all we need to do is see that the equation we create is completely within our control. That is, our credit card, our bank account, the nation's wealth, the world's wealth, is equal to— something. A *number* (the credit card, the bank account, the national wealth, etc.) which is assigned through some arbitrary means that is structured to look concrete, is equal to a *value*, which is also assigned by human beings.

In the case of our financial transactions, in the case of our economic equation, we can drop the physical aspect of what the number represents.In reality, this happened a long time ago; we dropped the physical aspect of what your credit card or bank account represents. So, let's forget what is "supposed" to be in the bank; it's not really there, anyway. All the bank has are numbers. They don't have any rocks, or gold, or anything like that.

Just as humans at one time assumed that the earth was the center of the universe, we assumed that we needed to think of money as something real. Today we know that atoms are composed mostly of empty space, that what keeps us from falling through the chairs we're sitting on is not the solidity of our clothes or of our bodies, but the electromagnetic charge of the atoms in us and in the chairs.

119

This is a remarkably abstract, yet remarkably real example, and one that we certainly don't think of when we sit down on a chair. And once you know that, you probably still won't think of that as the reason you're not falling through the chair in which you are sitting.

Once we learned that, we didn't start falling through the chairs. In the same way, once we recognize that money is a completely abstract concept, a thought, with only the value that we assign to it, the interactions between people will not stop.

When we played the game Monopoly, within the world of the game we assigned the value to the money that was printed on its face. Today, when someone purchases a car, we assign a value to his money in the same way we assigned a value to the Monopoly money. That is the agreed upon non-reality in which we live, and it's time to realize that.

There have been many attempts throughout the measured, recorded history of civilization by groups that tried to form models of a "utopian" society. The definitions of utopia varied with each group, but often the idea was somewhat similar to the type of society that one might believe is implied in this book. That is, what has been discussed here is removing the abstract, artificial conditions on human interactions—the conditions that have invariably laid the foundations for rigidly inequitable structures, structures in which humans are constrained from living the lives which they would naturally be living without such conditions.

All of these "utopian" societies have failed miserably, so that we have come to view the very word utopia with disdain and use it with a tinge of sarcasm. But there have been many societies in which this very socio-economic structure flourished for some time. One of the problems has been that the functioning, the maintenance of the group, just didn't work.

Another problem, as we all can easily imagine, is that often power and control become issues. As groups come together to form ever-larger groups, a certain degree of control becomes necessary, and that control takes the form of a government. That governing institution may function in the people's best interest, or it may begin, at some point, to come under the control of an unscrupulous individual, or individuals, who finds a way to have a disproportionate amount of resources—of things of value—for himself or herself.

Someone gets greedy.

We have often come to think that we cannot trust each other, that we (human beings) need to be organized in a manner that allows an institution—a government—to regulate our society. This has worked out fairly well in many aspects of our lives. A far lower percentage of people die of violence today than a century ago.

As this societal structure evolved, however, many societies came to be ruled by people whose only goal was to accumulate more wealth, more power, more control for themselves and their families. In today's world this wealth has become controlled by ever-smaller numbers of people.

There have always been a certain number of people, however, who have a true wish to help structure societies in a manner that will benefit the maximum number of people possible, just as there have been those whose only goal is to benefit themselves (and those with whom they work closely).

The failure of the utopian societies mentioned here has come about either because of a failure to organize in a sustainable manner, or due to the unscrupulous people within the groups, or those who have come to power over the groups. The fact that this has happened in certain societies, and the fact that we are aware of this, should give us the clear guidance that we need to control the governance of our own modern societies.

Everybody wants more. Some want a lot more.

We live in a time of abundance and technological breakthroughs to greater productivity andproblem solving. That is why everyone can have more.

Some of the governments of today have a genuine selfless goal of bettering the lives of the people whom they serve. With the interconnectedness of today's world, we are reaching a "tipping point" at which we can allow the true basic goodness that is inherent in the human character to steer our societies toward the goal of a life in which people can continue to evolve, without the absurd burdens of the abstract financial structures that prevent us from moving forward—just as gravity prevented us from leaving the earth until we developed the technology to break free.

In case you are worried about your house, your car, your chef-grade cookware, your other possessions—let me be clear: The idea of ownership is not being questioned here. The idea of what ownership is actually based upon is being questioned. The representational basis of money, and what that representation means, in terms of actual functioning, in terms of the use of objects and services, is being questioned.

So, this theory of economic relativity is not saying that you must share your shoes, your clothes, your car, or your house with someone else. The redistribution of wealth was part of the economic ideas attempted some places; we are not talking about the redistribution of wealth. The idea here is that wealth is an outdated concept, that there are enough shoes, enough clothes, enough cars, and enough housing in the world for everyone to be able to lead a comfortable, functional life.

The website everydollar.com reported a study by researchers at Harvard, UBC and Simon Fraser University. "Participants were given either $5 or $20 and asked to spend it by the end of the day. Half had to spend the money on themselves while the other half had to spend it on someone else." Those who spent the money on others were happier at the end of the day.

In another study conducted a few years ago of social behavior involving economics people were given $20 and told they had to share a portion of the money with another person. The amount that they shared was their decision, but the other person had to accept the money, or neither got to keep the money. They could have given the other person one or two dollars, but the average amount shared was $8.50.

I am not proposing you must share your food. There is enough food.

What is your money worth?

I would like to know: What is money for? Why do we need it?

Don't panic. I recognize that today, we still need money.

You bought this book, and paid for it with money; some version of paper or an electronic pulsethat our system accepts. A number. And that's fine for the time being; we all need money to eat, to pay the rent or mortgage, or to buy the next book.

But if we could structure an imaginary society in which people don't need or use money, there is absolutely no underlying reason why that society would not work.

This would not have been a realistic concept a hundred years ago, or even fifty years ago, before the advent of the communication software and devices that people are beginning to use, and which are advancing at a faster rate than most people are able to keep up with. Now that we are aware that we can point a smart phone at an item in a store and transfer money from our bank account or from our credit card account to purchase that item, we should be enlightened to what is really taking place and what each transaction represents.

And once we become aware of what those transactions represent, we should have a clear vision of the potential to free ourselves from something so abstract that we really no longer make the mental connection between the act and the supposed "reality" of cash. And we've talked about the fact that even hard cash is only an abstract entity, that cash represents something.

It's time to recognize that we don't need to tie those numbers on the microchip to another abstract entity such as numbers in a bank. *We*, the people of the world, are assigning value to those numbers in the bank. *We* are saying that the paper (cash) represents something of a certain value. *We*, through people who *represent* us, give value and credence to all things. Even in societies that are ruled by despotic rulers, those rulers still act as representatives of the people of the country, though not in a positive way. That is, even if the people ruling a country are not true representatives of the people living in the country, they are always viewed as such.

That which connects the abstract act of moving numbers on a microchip to our ability to obtain the physical things that support our lives is our good will… our belief. The belief is in a government that assigns and supports that which the numbers represent. And, at least in the view of most people in the world today, the government is, after all, the people.

125

21

Beyond the Numbers

We are quickly approaching a point in the development of human life when people will be living much longer, healthier lives. How will societies address this issue within the current economic systems? Will we expect people to work into their 100s? If not, how will society care for everyone? Let's be clear about whom we are talking: we are talking about you! Would you prefer to be euthanized, or perhaps just "allowed" to die without the care that you will not be able to afford when you reach 110 years old?

We, the people, are fast approaching a point in our civilization when we must be able to function without these artificial constraints. We can take the next step in representative financial actions by eliminating that aspect of such transactions that we have tended to identify as the most substantial—the most worldly, the most real—but which is, in fact, the most abstract of all:

Money, itself.

How will we do anything? How will a person buy a car or a house? How will we buy food? The answer we might like: go into the supermarket and pick out the food you want. But why would the farmer grow the food? It's obviously not that simple.

But this drastically new manner of functioning cannot happen overnight. Certainly, if we just expected people to do the work needed without reward, at first things would begin to fall apart, before we got motivated to start making things function again.

The necessary and required role for government

We need governments, which represent us, to begin to guide the societies of the world into this new paradigm.

Yet the shape of governments has changed radically over a relatively brief period of time. In today's world most of us assume that good governments are formed "deriving their just powers from the consent of those governed" (from the Declaration of Independence in 1776). The idea that those who governed were empowered by the "consent of those governed" was an extremely radical concept. It implied that power was not inherent in owning property or any other form of wealth, but was inherent in every person in the society, who in turn had the right and the ability to select whom they chose to make the decisions that affected their lives; in other words, to operate the government. At that time, of course, the reality was that power was inherent only in some people, but the foundation of the concept of true equality and empowerment was there.

In fact, very large numbers of people were not even thought of or included in the ideas of that Declaration; but we are continually working to achieve a better equality in which the idea of "those governed" actually includes all people.

We may take a step back for every couple of steps forward, but hopefully we will keep moving in the right direction.

We went from wealth—possessions—or heredity as the determining factor in the control of a nation (a group of people), to the idea that those who controlled—or governed—a nation did so by virtue of the people who lived in that nation, the people who were giving them the temporary authority to govern. Those governing were then said to "represent" the rest of the people, and did so only by their "consent."

It is an underlying assumption in such a system—some form of democratic government—that every action taken by those in positions of power is taken for the benefit of the people of that nation.

Yet, today it has become more and more obvious that those in control of many major industrial nations have come to make their decisions on the basis of the dictates of large financial institutions. The taxes imposed on people, the services provided by the governments, the health care of the population, support for the disadvantaged and he elderly—decisions about these crucial human issues are often determined to a large extent by people thinking in terms of their own status and finances.

If any country truly derives its "just powers from the consent of those governed", as the Declaration of Independence asserts, we must acknowledge that the most fundamental of those powers is what we call the money, finances, currency, etc. of that nation. The currency, representing the wealth of the nation, is given value by its people, who allow themselves to be governed. We allow those who govern to establish arbitrary rules that determine the structure of what our money means.

That meaning has become less and less substantial, less and less real. In looking outside ourselves for guidance in regulating our lives—a necessary principle to maintain a functional system—we have allowed a system to evolve which is so cumbersome, so convoluted, that the actual purpose of the system has been subverted into a vehicle that benefits a small group of people rather than those who give that group their power.

22

We, the People

We, the people of this country and this world, are constantly changing and creating new paradigms, new lenses through which we view the world. It is time to slowly, carefully, free ourselves from the artificially-imposed structure that requires us to use one very abstract object to represent another idea. It is time to let go of the previously essential, yet ultimately abstract and meaningless entity represented by what we refer to as "money," and begin lives that bring us to our full potential.

A transformation such as this would need to be far-reaching and to saturate the world's population. One individual or group cannot escape from a system or create a new system. What is needed is a larger transformational move.

The first step to this new economic order has begun with something that we have come to view as leading to a paradigm which appears to be quite different than the order being discussed here. In recent years the term "globalization" has come to be used to apply to something perhaps better described as "corporatization." With the corporatization of the financial world, by which we mean control by corporations, the financial structure has begun to transcend individual cultures. Corporate societies have become global. True globalization has the potential to be transformative.

Since corporations in today's world actually rule (much as nations ruled in the past), the most significant competition—the battles and wars—that are being fought in the world today are not being fought over land, but over economic power. What is it that runs a country? How is a country controlled in today's world? It is no longer the political dynamics of the government of a country that truly direct the country anymore. Every country in the world quails at the responses of financial markets to the actions of that nation. The manner in which the financial markets react determines, many times, what the country will do.

The ideals on which people believe that their nations are built have been relegated to a supporting role—as long as those ideals can be presented to appear in harmony with the economic perspectives of financial markets. Although the idea of fighting to support one's ideals or territory still exists, the real battles today are almost always over money. The battles are for representational values; that electronic number in the computer.

Let us hope.

Because, although this structure has evolved and been promoted from the beginning of civilization, and although it is anathema to what is being discussed in this treatise, the potential exists for this structure to be used to achieve that towards which the world is inevitably moving.

Today's distorted financial structure can lead—and has begun to lead—to a true globalization, a connection between the various peoples of the earth that erases geographical boundaries. Many of the real borders that exist today are not the national geographic borders that divide masses of land or property, but, are imaginary borders that have been established by corporations. (Even in the case of countries that control every aspect of their finances, these finances are still affected by corporations in other locations.) And remember—although it is the sovereign nation-states that recognize and give credence to these corporations, the corporations have managed to establish themselves as entities that are fluid enough to register their abstract home in any geographic location that works to their best advantage.

There are no true borders anymore between states, only between corporations. And even the reality of those borders depends on our perceptions. The most important wars are no longer fought over land, but rather over economic structure, since the economics are there to take care of the world. When coupled with the connectivity that the internet—and the realization of the extent to which we live in an interconnected world—has brought, we see that we are naturally being led to a true "globalization" that benefits all the peoples of the world.

Just as cities evolved into nation-states and nations-states evolved into countries, which in turn evolved into larger nations, today those nations are actually unable to truly enforce boundaries between different communities and different groups. We can adopt the positive elements of what has been happening through this overwhelming globalization (the dissolution of borders and the interconnectivity) and eliminate the negative sides (the conflicts of money and space).

Through this paradigm we have begun to see the world as an interdependent entity, comprised of us all and everything with which we are in touch; this is how the word "globalization" should be interpreted. We have fought over land, but we don't need to fight over economic structure. Economically, if we handle things correctly, we can manage the interactions within the world (currently viewed as financial transactions) without the types of battles that took place over land.

The idea that we have the power to shape the "economic" future is no longer a crazy dream: events all over the world are proving that the future is in our hands. And when I say, "In our hands", it is not a figurative or abstract statement, or as ephemeral as money. You have in your hands a cell phone with more computing power than anything that was imaginable in a computer the size of a building just a few years ago.

The paradigm shift being discussed here is not something that will happen tomorrow. There seem to be two competing trends in today's world: 1) more power moving towards large numbers of people or 2) more power moving towards a small number of people. We have significant choices to make.

Before too long, medical science and the connected technology will advance to the point that you, yes you, will be able to live to be 150 or 200 or 300. Even if the cost of medical treatment is affordable, the economy of each country will change as huge numbers of people are now much older.

Simultaneous to the much greater number of people living and living longer in the future, more and more of the engines of the economy will be provided by technology and artificial intelligence. The number of jobs will not match the income needs of the population. We must change the economic structure for our world to continue. We must find a way.

Whichever choice we make, whichever way the change happens, it will happen. It might be 300 years from now before "money" disappears, or it might be 100 years from now. But taking into consideration the exponential rates of change in so many fields, it may happen a lot sooner than we think.

The world is changing. Let's change it in the best way.

"You may say I'm a dreamer,
but I'm not the only one…"

— John Lennon *Imagine*

Special thanks to Ellen Raff and Kim Schlossberg for their help in making this book come to fruition.

After graduating from the University of Texas at Austin, William Bernstein lived in India before returning to his hometown of Dallas, Texas.

Bernstein now works at a nonprofit agency assisting survivors of human rights abuses. He has served as co-chair of a national coalition of experts and advocates who work with survivors of human trafficking. He ran for Congress and played in the World Series of Poker.